Indian Territorial Army and Women

Indian Territorial Army and Women

Kush Kalra

(Petitioner in the Case before the Court)

Vij Books India Pvt Ltd

New Delhi (India)

Published by

Vij Books India Pvt Ltd
(Publishers, Distributors & Importers)
2/19, Ansari Road
Delhi – 110 002
Phones: 91-11-43596460, 91-11-47340674
Mob: 9811094883
e-mail: contact@vijpublishing.com

Copyright © 2022, *Kush Kalra*

ISBN: 978-93-93499-01-1 (Hardback)
ISBN: 978-93-93499-02-8   (Paperback)
ISBN: 978-93-93499-03-5 (ebook)

Dedicated to

My Parents

Mr. Vijay Kalra & Mrs. Nirdosh Kalra

Brother & Sister in Law

Mr. Luv Kalra & Ms. Anita Kalra

and

My wife

Ms. Bhanu Tanwar Kalra

Contents

Chapter -1

Introduction

The Britishers raised the Territorial Army (TA) in 1920 through the Indian Territorial Act of 1920 and it was organised into two wings namely –'The Auxiliary Force' for Europeans & Anglo Indians and 'The Indian Territorial Force' for Indian Volunteers.

After Independence, the Territorial Act was passed in 1948, and the Territorial Army was formally inaugurated by the First Indian Governor General Shri C. Rajagopalachari on 9 October 1949. This Day is being celebrated as Prime Minister's TA Day Parade Every Year. Section 6 of the Territorial Army Act, 1948 provides for eligibility for enrolment to Territorial Army. It provides "Any person who is a citizen of India may offer himself for enrolment in the Territorial Army, and may, if he satisfies the prescribed conditions, be enrolled for such period and subject to such conditions as may be prescribed".

The Territorial Army is part of the regular army. Its present role is to relieve the Regular Army from static duties and assist the civil administration in dealing with natural calamities and maintenance of essential services in situations where the life of the communities is affected or the security of the country is threatened and to provide units for Regular Army as and when required.

Further to this is, it was mentioned on the Territorial Army Website at that time that "Presently the Territorial Army has a strength of 40000 persons comprising of Departmental TA units such as Railway, IOC, ONGC, Telecommunication and General Hospital and the non Departmental TA units of Infantry Bn (TA) and Ecological Bn (TA) affiliated to various infantry regiments".

The present role of the Territorial Army is to relieve the Regular Army from static duties and assist civil administration in dealing with natural calamities and maintenance of essential services in situations where like of the communities is affected or the security of the country is threatened, and to provide units for the Regular Army as an when required.

*It is pertinent to mention here that presently only **Male Candidates**[1] who are gainfully employed and are aged between 18-42 years of age or **Male Ex-Serviceman** who are medically fit are only eligible to apply for Territorial Army and the role of Territorial Army is such that without the assistance of **Females** it is unlikely that roles and responsibilities as mentioned above will be fulfilled as required.*

Territorial Army allows only "**Male Citizens** of India and **Ex-service officers** who are medically fit and are gainfully employed in Centre/ State Govt./Semi Govt./Pvt. Sector/Self Employed. It is pertinent to mention here that only **Male** Ex-Service officers can apply for the territorial army as per the recruitment rules of the Territorial Army, leaving no scope for **Female** Ex-Service officers.

The **Territorial Army** (**TA**) is a second line of defence after the Regular Indian Army; it is not a profession, occupation or a source of employment. It is only meant for those people who are already in mainstay civilian professions; in fact, gainful employment or self-employment in a civil profession is a prerequisite for joining the Territorial Army. Volunteers of the Territorial Army usually serve in uniform for 2–3 months every year, so that they can bear arms for national defence in times of dire need or national emergencies.

The Territorial Army has a strength of approximately 40,000 first-line troops (and 160,000 second line troops) comprising departmental Territorial Army units such as railway, IOCL, ONGC, telecommunication and General Hospital, and the non-departmental

---

1 Before 5th Jan, 2018 only male candidates were allowed in Territorial army, but now after the judgment of Delhi High Court even Females are allowed in Territorial army Link: https://www.livemint.com/ Politics/ E9KDl55yYL62W2GLzWxnOP/Delhi-HC-paves-way-for-recruitment-of-women-in-Territorial-A.html

Territorial Army units of infantry battalions and ecological battalions affiliated to various infantry regiments.

The TA units were actively involved in 1962, 1965 and 1971 operations. The "Terriers" have also taken part in OP-PAWAN in Srilanka, OP RAKSHAK in Punjab & J&K, OP RHINO and OP BAJRANG in North East in a most active manner. Departmental units came to the aid of the civil authorities during Industrial unrest and natural calamities, most famous being earthquake in Latoor (Maharastra), Uttarkashi in Garhwal Himalaya and the Super Cyclone in Orissa. The Ecological units have arrested man-made environmental degradation by planting 2.5 crore trees over 20,000 hectares of land in Mussoorie Hills & Pithoragarh (UP), Bikaner & Jaisalmer (Rajasthan) and ravines of Chambal in Madhya Pradesh.

Men of TA have taken active part in various adventure activities, famous one being scaling of Mt Tengchen Khang (6010 Mtr) in West Sikkim by Jt-Indo-British TA Mountaineering Expedition in May 98. The officer and men of the Territorial Army have been decorated for their gallantry and distinguished services. So for they have earned 02 Ati Vishisht Seva Medal (AVSM), 15 VSM, 05 Vir Chakra, 13 Sena Medal, 25 Mentioned-in-Despatches and 43 COAS commendation card.

The officers and men of the Territorial Army have been decorated for their gallantry and distinguished services. So far they have earned 01 Kirti Chakra, 05 Ati Vishisht Seva Medal, 05 Vir Chakra, 05 Shourya Chakra, 01 Yudh Seva Medal, 74 Sena Medal, 28 Vishist Seva Medal, 17 Mention-in-Dispatches and 266 Chief of the Army Staff Commendation Cards.

Many Industrialists, politicians and eminent personalities have been members of the TA. The force also has had the honour of appointing 11 officers over the years as Hony ADC to the President of India.

Ecological TA

There are ten ecological TA battalions which are sponsored by various state governments. TA Battalions use the technical expertise of the respective State Forest Department (SFD), for afforestation

3

related activities, Soil Conservation to promote the environment.

Background

The early eighties were a trying and testing time for the fragile ecology of the Shivalik Ranges. The Queen of Hills-Mussorie was on the brink of losing its pristine splendour due to the unscientific and illegal mining of limestone. The unorganised mining activity in the area, intensified the rate of deforestation in an unprecedented manner.

Alarmed at the ecological degradation in the Shivaliks, Dr Norman Borlough, from Wheat and Maize Centre, Mexico suggested to the former Prime Minister of India, Late Mrs. Indira Gandhi to involve the Indian Army to restore the ecological balance on a war footing. As the regular Army could not be utilised for the purpose, it was decided that a Territorial Army Unit be raised for the purpose, enrolling ex-servicemen from the region.

This was with the dual aim of re-settlement of Ex-Servicemen and regeneration of ecology. As an unique experiment 127 Infantry Battalion (Territorial Army) GARHWAL RIFLES was raised on 01 December 1982.

Concept

Ecological Task Force (ETF) Battalions (TA) have been raised to execute specific ecology related projects, with military like work culture and commitment, by enrolling Ex-Servicemen. ETF Battalions (TA) use technical expertise of the respective State Forest Department (SFD), for afforestation related activities and promote environment.

Present Status

Presently nine such Infantry Battalions (TA) Ecological, comprising 22 operational companies, are carrying out afforestation in difficult and degraded areas in States of Uttarakhand, Rajasthan, J & K, Himachal Pradesh, Delhi, Assam and Maharashtra. The Ecological Bn for Maharashtra has been raised in 2017 for the drought hit Marathwada region of the state. Also, a Composite Ecological

Task Force for National Mission for Clean Ganga is under raising at Allahabad. On completion of raising, one company each will be deployed at Kanpur, Varanasi and Allahabad for the said mission. ETF Bns are either funded by Min of Environment, Forest and Climate Change (MoEF & CC) or by respective State Govts. These ETF Battalions have been raised with the twin objectives of restoration of fragile ecosystem and affording excellent opportunity for Army Veterans to contribute in Nation building.

ETF Battalions have planted approximately 6.88 crore saplings and covered an area of 72,741 Hectares of land, with 75 to 80 percent of survival rate. ETF Battalions have been given due recognition for their exemplary contribution in the field of ecology and have been bestowed with various National and State level awards.

Initiative to Check Economic Migration along Border Areas

A unique initiative and vision of Indian Army has entailed plantation of high quality Walnut and Chilgoza saplings in Malari region of Uttrakhand to prevent migration of villagers. Malari region is strategically located in Niti Valley, on an axis leading to the China Border and is remotely located and cut off from Joshimath due to heavy snowfall between December-April. The locals migrate to lower regions during this period. There are no avenues of employment & even the cultivable land is inadequate for a sustainable livelihood. The project has been initiated on the directions of General Bipin Rawat, UYSM, AVSM, YSM, SM, VSM, ADC, Chief of the Army Staff, who conceived the idea and is the driving force behind the initiative.

The uniqueness of the initiative is that it involves all resident families in planting saplings of Walnut & Chilgoza, which will belong to them, and they would be sole beneficiaries of the fruits borne by the saplings planted by them.

The first phase of this pilot project was inaugurated at Malari on 19 May 2017. A large number of enthusiastic villagers attended the event and 4000 saplings of Walnut & Chilgoza were planted. In Phase II approximate 1,00,000 saplings will be planted over the next three years.

127 Inf Bn (TA) Eco, GARH RIF and 130 Inf Bn (TA) Eco, KUMAON have been earmarked for this project. The units have already prepared nurseries and sowed more than one lakh seedlings of Walnut specially procured from Central Institute for Temperate Horticulture, Srinagar, J & K. These saplings thereafter will be transplanted in designated areas of Garhwal and Kumaon region.

By virtue of their task and role, the Ecological Territorial Army units are contributing immensely by ecological activities towards disaster mitigation and also be part of Nation building efforts of the Indian Army.

During national emergency and natural calamities, these Territorial Army personnel are embodiment in which they are liable to perform the assigned duties. The TA personnel of these units perform the same task which they do in their parent department, i.e. in IOC/ Indian Railways/ ONGC/

Oil Sector (TA) Units

The Assam agitation of 1980, resulted in colossal loss of oil production estimated at over Rs 5000/- crores, Combat Engineer Regiments were deployed to take over the Oil and Gas installations to maintain production. Raising of the Oil Sector (TA) units was the result of the lessons learnt due to this Oil Ops. Accordingly, a proposal was initiated by the then Min of Chemical & Fertilizer (Now Min Petroleum and Natural Gas) for raising of Territorial Army Battalions, separately for all the three fields of Oil industry ie Exploration, Refining and Marketing. The proposal was accepted and the raising of the following three Oil Sector (TA) units were approved by the Ministry of Defence.

- 801 Engineer Regt (TA) Refinery & Pipeline

- 811 Engineer Regiments Oil Natural Gas Corporation (TA)

- 414 ASC Battalion Marketing (TA)

These units have Territorial Army personnel enrolled from various fields of Oil Sector PSUs. During national emergency/ crises these Territorial Army personnel are embodied in which they are liable to perform the assigned duties. The task of Oil Sector (TA) units is more of technical in nature than of combat. The TA personnel of these units perform the same task which they do in their parent department i.e. in Oil Companies.

Women employees of Oil Sectors PSUs are also allowed to be commissioned/enrolled as Officer, Junior Commissioned Officer and Other Ranks in Oil Sector (TA) units as commensurate to civil ranks. Lt Shilpy Gargmukh who is an employee of ONGC, is the first lady officer of Oil Sector (PSU), who has been commissioned in 811 Engineer Regiment (TA) ONGC.

Railway Engineer Regiments (TA)

There are six Railway Engineer Regiments (TA):-

- 969 Railway Engineer Regiment (TA)
- 970 Railway Engineer Regiment (TA)
- 1031 Railway Engineer Regiment (TA)
- 1032 Railway Engineer Regiment (TA)
- 1101 Railway Engineer Regiment (TA)
- 1105 Railway Engineer Regiment (TA)

These units have Territorial Army personnel enrolled from various Railway Zones. During national emergency/crises these Territorial Army personnel are embodiment in which they are liable to perform the assigned duties. The TA personnel of these units perform the same task which they do in their parent department, i.e. in Railways.

Women employees of Railways are also allowed to be commissioned/ enrolled as Officer, Junior Commissioned Officer and Other Ranks in Railway Engineer Regiments (TA). Presently there are five women sappers enrolled with Railway Engineer Regiments (TA).

Chapter - 2

Males in Territorial Army

After Independence Territorial Act was passed in 1948 and the Territorial Army was formally inaugurated by the First Indian Governor General Shri C. Rajagopalachari on 9 October 1949. This Day is being celebrated as Prime Minister's TA Day Parade Every Year. Section 6 of the Territorial Army Act, 1948 provides for eligibility for **enrolment to Territorial Army**. It provides "Any person who is a citizen of India may offer himself for enrolment in the Territorial Army, and may, if he satisfies the prescribed conditions, be enrolled for such period and subject to such conditions as may be prescribed".

The Petitioner/Writer has come across the Territorial Army Recruitment Advertisement of 2015 which is marked as **Annexure - 1** and came to know that only **Male** Candidates and **Male** Ex-Service officers who are medically fit and who are gainfully employed and are aged between 18-42 years of age (as on the date of notification of territorial army advertisement) are only eligible to apply for Territorial Army Recruitment. As the recruitment rules for Territorial Army does not allow and Female Candidate who are Gainfully employed and aged between 18-42 years to apply for Territorial Army.

The recruitment rules of Territorial Army were in clear violation of Article 14, 15(1), 19(1)(g) and 21 of the Constitution of India.

Article 14 of the Constitution Of India

14. Equality before law The State shall not deny to any person equality before the law or the equal protection of the laws within the territory of India Prohibition of discrimination on grounds of religion, race, caste, sex or place of birth.

Article 15 of the Constitution Of India

15. Prohibition of discrimination on grounds of religion, race, caste, sex or place of birth

(1)   The State shall not discriminate against any citizen on grounds only of religion, race, caste, sex, place of birth or any of them

(2)   No citizen shall, on grounds only of religion, race, caste, sex, place of birth or any of them, be subject to any disability, liability, restriction or condition with regard to

(a)   access to shops, public restaurants, hotels and palaces of public entertainment; or

(b)   the use of wells, tanks, bathing ghats, roads and places of public resort maintained wholly or partly out of State funds or dedicated to the use of the general public

(3)   Nothing in this article shall prevent the State from making any special provision for women and children

(4)   Nothing in this article or in clause (2) of Article 29 shall prevent the State from making any special provision for the advancement of any socially and educationally backward classes of citizens or for the Scheduled Castes and the Scheduled Tribes

Article 19 of the Constitution Of India

19. Protection of certain rights regarding freedom of speech etc

(1)   All citizens shall have the right.

(a)   to freedom of speech and expression;

(b)   to assemble peaceably and without arms;

(c)   to form associations or unions;

(d)   to move freely throughout the territory of India;

(e)   to reside and settle in any part of the territory of India; and

(f)   omitted

(g)   to practise any profession, or to carry on any occupation, trade or business

(2)   Nothing in sub clause (a) of clause (1) shall affect the operation of any existing law, or prevent the State from making any law, in so far as such law imposes reasonable restrictions on the exercise of the right conferred by the said sub clause in the interests of the sovereignty and integrity of India, the security of the State, friendly relations with foreign States, public order, decency or morality or in relation to contempt of court, defamation or incitement to an offence.

(3)   Nothing in sub clause (b) of the said clause shall affect the operation of any existing law in so far as it imposes, or prevent the State from making any law imposing, in the interests of the sovereignty and integrity of India or public order, reasonable restrictions on the exercise of the right conferred by the said sub clause.

(4)   Nothing in sub clause (c) of the said clause shall affect the operation of any existing law in so far as it imposes, or prevent the State from making any law imposing, in the interests of the sovereignty and integrity of India or public order or morality, reasonable restrictions on the exercise of the right conferred by the said sub clause.

(5)   Nothing in sub clauses (d) and (e) of the said clause shall affect the operation of any existing law in so far as it imposes, or prevent the State from making any law imposing, reasonable restrictions on the exercise of any of the rights conferred by the said sub clauses either in the interests of the general public or for the protection of the interests of any Scheduled Tribe.

(6)   Nothing in sub clause (g) of the said clause shall affect the operation of any existing law in so far as it imposes, or prevent the State from making any law imposing, in the interests of the general public, reasonable restrictions on the exercise of the right conferred by the said sub clause, and, in particular, nothing in the said sub

clause shall affect the operation of any existing law in so far as it relates to, or prevent the State from making any law relating to,

(i)   the professional or technical qualifications necessary for practising any profession or carrying on any occupation, trade or business, or

(ii)   the carrying on by the State, or by a corporation owned or controlled by the State, of any trade, business, industry or service, whether to the exclusion, complete or partial, of citizens or otherwise

Article 21 of the Constitution of India

21. Protection of life and personal liberty No person shall be deprived of his life or personal liberty except according to procedure established by law

> The description about Territorial Army in advertisement clearly indicated that the work performed by Territorial army is for civilian good and by not allowing females to be a part of Territorial Army the army recruitment is acting unfair and bias towards whole female community. It is pertinent to mention that many Male industrialists, Male Politicians and Male eminent personalities have been member of Territorial Army.

The eligibility criteria for Territorial Army clearly mentions that "only those male candidates who are gainfully employed are eligible for Territorial Army" This means a Male person who may be employed in Government Service, A Legal Practitioner, A Doctor, A Engineer, Paying Guest Owner, Farmer or Businessman is eligible to apply for territorial army if he is gainfully employed and is aged between 18-42 years of age as on the date of notification for Territorial Army Recruitment.

It is pertinent to mention that many **Male** industrialists, politicians and eminent personalities have been member of Territorial Army. Navdeep Singh, a lawyer, is known to have received the highest number of decorations/awards in the Territorial Army. Mohanlal, the Malayalam Film Superstar is a Lt Col in the TA (Madras Regiment). Even Male Honorary officers have been appointed by Territorial

Army like Kapil Dev, Mahendra Singh Dhoni and Abhinav Bindra[1].

On every Republic Day parade, the Indian Government is proud to showcase "women power" but in reality, the picture is entirely different. The women officers are still not allowed to join combat units unlike in the countries like Israel and United States and neither allowed in NDA. In the United States, women were allowed in combat roles as recently as in 2013 after it lifted the 1994 Ban on women in direct combat roles. In 1995, Norway became the first country to allow women to serve on submarines. Russian women have been fighting in combat since World War 1 and in fact no role in the Soviet military was closed for women including sniper duties, machine gunners, tanks and fighter pilots etc.

No doubt, India took a major step in allowing women to apply for the Armed Forces but the country is still lagging behind from many other countries in having women in command of military units.

Under Article 14 of the Constitution of India, every citizen has the right to equality of law and equal protection before law. The concept of an arbitrary action being in violation of Article 14 was first introduced in the case of E.P. Royappa v. State of Tamil Nadu, (1974) 4 SCC 3, wherein it was observed that 'equality is antithetic to arbitrariness'. Thus Article 14 has a very wide ambit and encompasses within it equality, the principles of natural justice and is a mandate against arbitrary state actions. This imposes a duty on the state to act fairly. Good governance in conformity with the mandate of Article 14, "raises a reasonable or legitimate expectation in every citizen to be treated fairly in its interaction with the state and its instrumentalities."[2]

India being a developing country in order to develop needs the tool of women empowerment more than anything. Conferment of equal status on women apart from being a constitutional right has been recognized as a human right. In the words of Kofi Annan - "There is no tool more effective than the empowerment of women for

---

1   Source Link : https://en.wikipedia.org/wiki/Territorial_Army_(India)

2   (Ref: Food Corporation of India. v. Kamdhenu Cattlefeed Industries Reported in (1993) 1 SCC 71)

development of a country."

Inequalities between the two sexes and discrimination against women have also been long-standing issues all over the world. Thus, women's pursuit of equality with man is a universal phenomenon.

Chapter -3

Women Barred from Entry in Territorial Army

Lord Denning in his book "Due Process of Law", has observed about women in the following words: "A woman feels as keenly, thinks as clearly, as a man. She in her sphere does work as useful as man does in his. She has as much right to her freedom - to develop her personality to the full as a man. When she marries, she does not become the husband's servant but his equal partner. If his work is more important in life of the community, her's is more important of the family. Neither can do without the other. Neither is above the other or under the other. They are equals."

The Petitioner/Writer has come across the Territorial Army Recruitment Advertisement of 2015 which is marked as Annexure-1 and came to know that females who are gainfully employed and medically fit are not eligible to apply for Territorial Army Recruitment which according to the petitioner was violative of their fundamental rights under Indian Constitution.

The Constitution of India intended to apply equality amongst men and women in all spheres of life. Article 14 of the Indian Constitution talks about equality. It provides that State shall not deny to any person equality before law or the equal protection of laws within the territory of India. Article 15(1) of the Indian Constitution provides that "the State shall not discriminate against any citizen on grounds only of religion, race, caste, sex, place of birth or any of them " . Article 39 A in Part IV of the Constitution deals with Directive Principles of State Policy which provides that the State shall direct its policies towards securing that the citizens, **men and women** equally, have the right to adequate means of livelihood.

In the case of **Charu Khurana vs Union of India**, 2012 (12) SCALE701 the question for consideration before the Supreme Court was whether the female artists who are eligible, can be deprived to work in the film industry as make-up-man and only be permitted to work as hair dressers, solely because the Association, the Respondent No.5—Cine Costume Make up Artists and Hair Dressers Association which was controlled by the Trade union Act, 1926 has incorporated a clause relating to this kind of classification and also further stipulated that a person to work must be a resident of of Maharashtra for a period of five years and nonchalantly stood embedded on its stand. Court quashed the said clauses and further directed the petitioner (Charu Khurana) shall be registered as member of the 5th respondent.

In the often-cited judgment titled C.B. Muthamma, I.F.S. v. Union of India & Ors.[1], a challenge was laid by a senior member of the Indian Foreign Services complaining of hostile discrimination against women in the service. Rule 8 of the Indian Foreign Service (Conduct and Discipline) Rules, 1961 which required a woman member of the service to mandatorily obtain permission of the government, in writing, before her marriage was solemnized was assailed by the petitioner. This rule also prescribed that any time after the marriage, "a woman member of the service may be required to resign from service", if the government was satisfied that her family and domestic commitments are likely to come in the way of the due and efficient discharge of her duties as a member of the service. On the petitioner's challenge to this rule as being violative of Articles 14 and 16 of the Constitution of India, the Supreme Court, in the judgment penned by Krishna Iyer, Judge for the Bench, observed as follows:

"At the first blush this rule is in defiance of Article 16. If a married man has a right, a married woman, other things being equal, stands on no worse footing. This misogynous posture is a hangover of the masculine culture of manacling the weaker sex forgetting how our struggle for national freedom was also a battle against woman's thraldom. Freedom is indivisible, so is Justice. That our founding

---

1   1979 AIR 1868, 1980 SCR (1) 668

faith enshrined in Articles 14 and 16 should have been tragically ignored vis-à-vis half of India's humanity viz. our women, is a sad reflection on the distance between Constitution in the book and law in action. And if the executive as the surrogate of Parliament, makes rules in the teeth of Part III (fundamental rights) especially when high political office, even diplomatic assignment has been filled by women, the inference of die hard allergy to gender parity is inevitable.

Men and women are equal in all occupations and all situations, the sensitivities of sex or the peculiarities of societal sectors or the handicaps of either sex may compel selectivity. But save where the differentiation is demonstrable, the rule of equality must govern."

In the case of Anuj Garg & Ors. v. Hotel Association of India & Ors.[2] , the Supreme Court was concerned with a challenge to the Constitutional validity of Section 30 of the Punjab Excise Act, 1914 which prohibited employment of "any man under the age of 25 years" or "any woman" in any part of such premises in which liquor or intoxicating drugs were consumed by the public. The challenge had commenced by way of a writ petition, filed under Article 226 of the Constitution of India before a Division Bench of High court in which the court had declared the statutory provision as ultra vires Articles 19(1)(g), 14 and 15 of the Constitution of India to the extent that it prohibited employment of any woman in any part of such premises, in which liquor or intoxicating drugs were consumed by the public. The decision was challenged before the Supreme Court, which, while repelling the challenge, upheld the judgment holding that prohibition from employment avenues in bars etc. was oppressive and violated the rights of the women. Some observations of the court were:

"When a discrimination is sought to be made on the purported ground of classification, such classification must be founded on a rational criteria. The criteria which in absence of any constitutional provision and, it will bear repetition to state, having regard to the societal conditions as they prevailed in early 20th century, may not

2   Appeal (civil) 5657 of 2007

16

be a rational criteria in the 21st century. In the early 20th century, the hospitality sector was not open to women in general. In the last 60 years, women in India have gained entry in all spheres of public life. They have also been representing people at grass root democracy. They are now employed as drivers of heavy transport vehicles, conductors of service carriages, pilots, etc. Women can be seen to be occupying Class IV posts to the post of a Chief Executive Officer of a multinational company. They are now widely accepted both in police as also army services."

In *Babita Puniya v. The Secretary & Anr.*[3] the court had ruled on a challenge to the denial of permanent commission only to women officers, who were commissioned into the Air Force and the Army in the Short Service Commission. The court had, inter alia observed that the women officials had undertaken the same training of one year as the male permanent commissioned officers whereas 10 batches of male short commissioned officers who had undergone training of much lesser period, of only three months, in the Air Force Administrative College were considered and granted permanent commission in the same period, when women short service commissioned officers continued to work in that capacity. So far as the areas of operation of Air Force where women should be employed was concerned, the court observed that it being a policy decision, this was an issue which was not for the court to decide. Furthermore, it was observed that the policy decision not to offer permanent commission to Short Service Commissioned officers across the board for men and women being on parity and as part of manpower management exercises, was a policy decision which was not required to be interfered with. The court, however, observed that the questions of suitability or requirement were not in doubt and that the advertisement issued by the respondents held out a promise to women Air Force officers for grant of permanent commission depending on two factors which were vacancy, position and suitability of the officer. The officers had thus joined the Air Force on the promise of these terms of recruitment apart from other conditions of service and the respondents could not introduce an

---

3   W.P.(C) No. 1597/2003

alien element other than these two elements. It therefore, ruled that the Short Service Commissioned officers of the Air Force who had opted for permanent commission and were not granted permanent commission but granted extension of Short Service Commissions, as well as those of the Army, were entitled to permanent commission at par with male Short Service Commissioned officers with all consequential benefits.

In *Annie Nagaraja & Ors. v. Union of India & Ors.*[4], whereby high court decided six writ petitions filed by 70 women officers who had joined Indian Navy as Short Service Commissioned officers in different branches which includes Education, Logistics and ATC seeking entitlement to permanent commission. In para 32 of the judgment, the court noted that the petitioners along with male officers had undertaken the same kind of training but nevertheless were denied permanent commission although the men were granted the permanent commission with no special merit except for the fact that they were males. It was held that this tantamounted to gender discrimination. The court held that the 2008 policy of the respondents which took no care to offer permanent commission to the women officers in the branches where these officers had worked as Short Service Commissioned officers for 14 years, was irrational and a clear case of discrimination and granted relief to the petitioners.

Despite Fundamental Right to Equality or Right to Practice any Profession, or to carry on any occupation, trade or business; discrimination against woman continued even in the acts of State like in Air India vs. Nargesh Mirza & Ors., AIR1981SC1829 where service regulations which provides for termination of service of female air hostesses after they attain 35 years of age or on marriage was held to be unconstitutional by Hon'ble Supreme Court.

Even the discriminatory practices in customs where women are not allowed to right of Inheritance of Property were dealt with by Courts and discriminatory practices were removed. In the case of *Nirmala and ors. Vs. Govt. of NCT of Delhi & ors.*, ILR(2010)Supp.(1)Delhi413 this Hon'ble Court has held that daughters are equally

---

4   MANU/DE/2573/2015

entitled to the Agricultural Property.

When discrimination is sought to be made on the purported ground of classification and such classification must be founded on a rational criteria. The criteria which in absence of any constitutional provision and it will bear repetition to state, having regard to the societal conditions as they prevailed in the early 20th century, may not be rational criteria in the 21st century.

In the last 75 years women in India have gained entry in all spheres of public life. They have also been representing people at grass root democracy. They are now employed as drivers of heavy transport vehicles, conductors of services carriage, pilots etc. All women can be seen to be occupying class IV posts, to the post of a Chief Executive Officer of a Multinational company and they are now widely accepted in both police and army services yet they face discrimination in appointment to various posts.

Chapter - 4

Constitution of India and Discrimination against Women

Gender equality and dignity for women, is an inalienable and inseparable part of the basic structure of the Constitution[1]. Since women transcend all social barriers, the most fundamental facet of equality under the Constitution is gender equality and gender equity. The Constitutional mandate to the State is that it shall not discriminate against any citizen on the grounds of sex and marital status. Therefore, the State has to treat women whether working or studying with the same yardstick and provide the same benefits and protection through a statutory and regulatory framework. This is the very spirit of equality enshrined under Article 14. The international instruments recognise and reiterate that the family is a natural and fundamental group unit of society; provide that it is the right of men and women of marriageable age to marry and found a family, and clearly state that such right is entitled to protection by society and the State.

The Indian Army is the land-based branch and the largest component of the Indian Armed Forces. The President of India is the Supreme Commander of the Indian Army. The primary mission of the Indian Army is to ensure national security and national unity, defend the nation from external aggression and internal threats, and maintain peace and security within its borders. In today's time, there is no

---

1   THE CONSTITUTION OF INDIA 1950, Article 15
    15. Prohibition of discrimination on grounds of religion, race, caste, sex or place of birth
    (3) Nothing in this article shall prevent the State from making any special provision for women and children

scope for discrimination on the ground of pregnancy/gender/ marriage and not allowing females or discriminating with them is violative of Constitution of India.

Article 14 of Indian Constitution aims to protect persons similarly placed against discriminatory treatment

While deciding about the constitutionality of a statute in the light of Article 14 of the Constitution of India, a Constitutional Bench of the Supreme Court, after referring the earlier judgments regarding the intelligible differentia, in its landmark judgment in Ram Krishna Dalmia v. Justice S.R. Tendolkar, AIR 1958 SC 538 has narrated the established principles as follows:

"The principle enunciated above has been consistently adopted and applied in subsequent cases. The decisions of this Court further establish-

(a) that a law may be constitutional even though it relates to a single individual if, on account of some special circumstances or reasons applicable to him and not applicable to others, that single individual may be treated as a class by himself;

(b) that there is always a presumption in favour of the constitutionality of an enactment and the burden is upon him who attacks it to show that there has been a clear transgression of the constitutional principles;

(c) that it must be presumed that the legislature understands and correctly appreciates the need of its own people, that its laws are directed to problems made manifest by experience and that its discriminations are based on adequate grounds;

(d) that the legislature is free to recognise degrees of harm and may confine its restrictions to those cases where the need is deemed to be the clearest;

(e) that in order to sustain the presumption of constitutionality the court may take into consideration matters of common knowledge, matters of common report, the history of the times and may assume every state of facts which can be conceived existing at the

21

time of legislation; and

(f) that while good faith and knowledge of the existing conditions on the part of a legislature are to be presumed, if there is nothing on the face of the law or the surrounding circumstances brought to the notice of the court on which the classification may reasonably be regarded as based, the presumption of constitutionality cannot be carried to the extent of always holding that there must be some undisclosed and un-known reasons for subjecting certain individuals or corporations to hostile or discriminating legislation."

In Ram Krishna Dalmia and Ors. vs. Shri Justice S.R. Tendolkar and Ors., AIR 1958 SC 538 the Hon'ble Apex Court considered the interplay of the doctrines of equality and classification and held:-

"It is now well established that while Article 14 forbids class legislation, it does not forbid reasonable classification for the purposes of legislation. In order, however, to pass the test of permissible classification two conditions must be fulfilled, namely (i) that the classification must be found on an intelligible differentia which distinguishes persons or things that are grouped together from others left out of the group, and (ii) that differentia must have a rational relation to the object sought to be achieved by the statute in question. The classification may be founded on different bases, namely, geographical, or according to objects or occupations or the like. What is necessary is that there must be a nexus between the basis of classification and the object of the Act under consideration. It is also well established by the decisions of Supreme Court that article 14 condemns discrimination not only by a substantive law but also by a law of procedure."

Speaking for the Court, Chief Justice S.R. Das enunciated some principles, which have been referred to and relied in all subsequent judgments. These are:

"(a) that a law may be constitutional even though it relates to a single individual if, on account of some special circumstances or reasons applicable to him and not applicable to others, that single individual may be treated as a class by himself;

(b) that there is always a presumption in favour of the constitutionality of an enactment and the burden is upon him who attacks it to show that there has been a clear transgression of the constitutional principles;

(c) that it must be presume that the legislature understands and correctly appreciates the need of its own people, that its laws are directed to problems made manifest by experience and that its discriminations are based on adequate grounds;

(d) that the legislature is free to recognize degrees of harm and may confine its restrictions to those cases where the need is deemed to be the clearest;

(e) that in order to sustain the presumption of constitutionality the Court may take into consideration matters of common knowledge, matters of common report, the history of times and may assume every state of facts which can be conceived existing at the time of legislation; and

(f) that while good faith and knowledge of the existing conditions on the part of a legislature are to be resumed, if there is nothing on the face of the law or the surrounding circumstances brought to the notice of the court on which the classification may reasonably be regarded as based, the presumption of constitutionality cannot be carried to the extent of always holding that there must be some undisclosed and unknown reasons for subjecting certain individuals or corporations to hostile or discriminating legislation."

In Probhudas Morarjee Rajkotia v. Union of India[2], a Constitutional Bench[3] of the Supreme Court, while interpreting Article 14 of the Constitution of India, held as follows:

2   AIR 1966 SC 1044

3   **Constitution bench** is the name given to the benches of the Supreme Court of India which consist of at least five judges of the court which sit to decide any case "involving a substantial question of law as to the interpretation" of the Constitution of India or "for the purpose of hearing any reference" made by the President of India under Article 143. This provision has been mandated by Article 145 (3) of the Constitution of India.

"It cannot be too strongly emphasized that to make out a case of denial of the equal protection of the laws under Art. 14 of the Constitution, a plea of differential treatment is by itself not sufficient. An applicant pleading that Article 14 has been violated must make out that not only he had been treated differently from other but he has been so treated from persons similarly circumstanced without any reasonable basis, and such differential treatment is unjustifiably made."

In Western M.P. Electric Power & Supply Co. Ltd. v. State of U.P., AIR 1970 SC 21, the Hon'ble Supreme Court held that Article 14 of the Constitution of India does not operate against rational classification. The relevant portion is as under:

"Article 14 of the Constitution ensures equality among equals; its aim is to protect persons similarly placed against discriminatory treatment. It does not, however, operate against rational classification. A person setting up a grievance of denial of equal treatment by law must establish that between persons similarly circumstanced, some were treated to their prejudice and the differential treatment had no reasonable relation to the object sought to be achieved by the law."

In Mohd. Shujat Ali vs. Union of India, 1975 (3) SCC 76, the Hon'ble Supreme Court observed that Article 14 ensures to every person equality before law and equal protection of the laws. However, the constitutional code of equality and equal opportunity does not mean that the same laws must be applicable to all persons. It does not compel the State to run "all its laws in the channels of general legislation". It recognises that having regard to differences and disparities which exist among men and things, they cannot all be treated alike by the application of the same laws. "To recognise marked differences that exist in fact is living law; to disregard practical differences and concentrate on some abstract identities is lifeless logic." The Legislature must necessarily, if it is to be effective at all in solving the manifold problems which continually come before it, enact special legislation directed towards specific ends limited in its application to special classes of persons or things. "Indeed, the greater part of all legislation is special, either in the extent to which it operates, or the objects sought to be attained by it." At the same time, the Court cautioned against the readymade invoking of the doctrine of classification to ward off every challenge to the legislative instruments on the ground of violation of equality clause and observed:

> *"The equal protection of the laws is a "pledge of the protection of equal laws". But laws may classify. And, as pointed out by Justice Brawer, "the very idea of classification is that of inequality". The Court has tackled this paradox over the years and in doing so, it has neither abandoned the demand for equality nor denied the legislative right to classify. It has adopted a middle course of realistic reconciliation. It has resolved the contradictory demands of legislative specialization and constitutional generality by a doctrine of reasonable classification. This doctrine recognises that the legislature may classify for the purpose of legislation but requires that the classification must be reasonable. It should ensure that persons or things similarly situated are all similarly treated. The measure of reasonableness of a classification is the degree of its success in treating similarly those similarly situated."*

> *"A reasonable classification is one which includes all persons or things similarly situated with respect to the purpose of the law. There should be no discrimination between one person or thing and another, if as regards the subject-matter of the legislation their position is substantially the same. This is sometimes epigrammatically described by saying that what the constitutional code of equality and equal opportunity requires is that among equals, the law should be equal and that like should be treated alike. But the basic principle underlying the doctrine is that the Legislature should have the right to classify and impose special burdens upon or grant special benefits to persons or things grouped together under the classification, so long as the classification is of persons or things similarly situated with respect to the purpose of the legislation, so that all persons or things similarly situated are treated alike by law. The test which has been evolved for this purpose is - and this test has been consistently applied by this Court in all decided cases since the commencement of the Constitution - that the classification must be founded on an*

intelligible differentia which distinguishes certain persons or things that are grouped together from others and that differentia must have a rational relation to the object sought to be achieved by the legislation."

In Mohd. Shujat Ali vs. Union of India, 1975 (3) SCC 76, the Hon'ble Supreme Court observed that:

Article 14 ensures to every person equality before law and equal protection of the laws. However, the constitutional code of equality and equal opportunity does not mean that the same laws must be applicable to all persons. It does not compel the State to run "all its laws in the channels of general legislation". It recognises that having regard to differences and disparities which exist among men and things, they cannot all be treated alike by the application of the same laws. "To recognise marked differences that exist in fact is living law; to disregard practical differences and concentrate on some abstract identities is lifeless logic." The Legislature must necessarily, if it is to be effective at all in solving the manifold problems which continually come before it, enact special legislation directed towards specific ends limited in its application to special classes of persons or things. "Indeed, the greater part of all legislation is special, either in the extent to which it operates, or the objects sought to be attained by it." At the same time, the Court cautioned against the readymade invoking of the doctrine of classification to ward off every challenge to the legislative instruments on the ground of violation of equality clause and observed:

"The equal protection of the laws is a "pledge of the protection of equal laws". But laws may classify. And, as pointed out by Justice Brawer, "the very idea of classification is that of inequality". The Court has tackled this paradox over the years and in doing so, it has neither abandoned the demand for equality nor denied the legislative right to classify. It has adopted a middle course of realistic reconciliation. It has resolved the contradictory demands of legislative specialization and constitutional generality by a doctrine of reasonable classification. This doctrine recognises that the legislature may classify for the purpose of legislation but requires that the classification must be reasonable. It should

ensure that persons or things similarly situated are all similarly treated. The measure of reasonableness of a classification is the degree of its success in treating similarly those similarly situated."

"A reasonable classification is one which includes all persons or things similarly situated with respect to the purpose of the law. There should be no discrimination between one person or thing and another, if as regards the subject-matter of the legislation their position is substantially the same. This is sometimes epigrammatically described by saying that what the constitutional code of equality and equal opportunity requires is that among equals, the law should be equal and that like should be treated alike. But the basic principle underlying the doctrine is that the Legislature should have the right to classify and impose special burdens upon or grant special benefits to persons or things grouped together under the classification, so long as the classification is of persons or things similarly situated with respect to the purpose of the legislation, so that all persons or things similarly situated are treated alike by law. The test which has been evolved for this purpose is - and this test has been consistently applied by Court in all decided cases since the commencement of the Constitution - that the classification must be founded on an intelligible differentia which distinguishes certain persons or things that are grouped together from others and that differentia must have a rational relation to the object sought to be achieved by the legislation."

A Constitutional Bench of the Hon'ble Supreme Court in D.S. Nakara v. Union of India, (1983) 1 SCC 305, explained the said concept of Article 14 of the Constitution of India, as follows:

"The decisions clearly lay down that though Article 14 forbids class legislation, it does not forbid reasonable classification for the purpose of legislation. In order, however, to pass the test of permissible classification, two conditions must be fulfilled viz. (i) that the classification must be founded on an intelligible differentia which distinguishes persons or things that are grouped together from those that are left out of the group; and (ii) that differentia must have a rational relation to the objects sought to be achieved by the statute

27

in question[4]. The classification may be founded on differential basis according to objects sought to be achieved but what is implicit in it is that there ought to be a nexus i.e. causal connection between the basis of classification and object of the statute under consideration. It is equally well settled by the decisions of Court that Article 14 condemns discrimination not only by a substantive law but also by a law of procedure.

Supreme Court speaking through Chandrachud, C.J. In re Special Courts Bill, 1978, AIR 1979 SC 478, restated the settled propositions which emerged from the judgments of Court undoubtedly insofar as they were relevant to the decision on the points arising for consideration in that matter. Four of them are apt and relevant for the present purpose and may be extracted. They are:

"***

(3) The constitutional command to the State to afford equal protection of its laws sets a goal not attainable by the invention and application of a precise formula. Therefore, classification need not be constituted by an exact or scientific exclusion or inclusion of persons or things. The courts should not insist on delusive exactness or apply doctrinaire tests for determining the validity of classification in any given case. Classification is justified if it is not palpably arbitrary.

(4) The principle underlying the guarantee of Article 14 is not that the same rules of law should be applicable to all persons within the Indian territory or that the same remedies should be made available to them irrespective of differences of circumstances. It only means that all persons similarly circumstanced shall be treated alike both in privileges conferred and liabilities imposed. Equal laws would have to be applied to all in the same situation, and there should be no discrimination between one person and another if as regards the subject-matter of the legislation their position is substantially the same.

***

---

4   See Ram Krishna Dalmia v. Justice S.R. Tendolkar, AIR 1958 SC 538

(6) The law can make and set apart the classes according to the needs and exigencies of the society and as suggested by experience. It can recognise even degree of evil, but the classification should never be arbitrary, artificial or evasive.

(7) The classification must not be arbitrary but must be rational, that is to say, it must not only be based on some qualities or characteristics which are to be found in all the persons grouped together and not in others who are left out but those qualities or characteristics must have a reasonable relation to the object of the legislation. In order to pass the test, two conditions must be fulfilled, namely, (1) that the classification must be founded on an intelligible differentia which distinguishes those that are grouped together from others and (2) that that differentia must have a rational relation to the object sought to be achieved by the Act."

In Sri Srinivasa Theatre and others vs. Government of Tamil Nadu and others, (1992) 2 SCC 643, while explaining the scope of Article 14, the Hon'ble Supreme Court at paragraph Nos. 9 and 10, held thus:-

"9. Article 14 of the Constitution enjoin upon the State not to deny to any person 'Equality before law' or 'the equal protection of laws' within the territory of India. The two expressions do not mean the same thing even if there may be much in common. Section 1 of the XIV Amendment to U.S. Constitution uses only the latter expression whereas the Irish Constitution (1937) and the West German Constitution (1949) use the expression "equal before law" alone. Both these expressions are used together in the Universal Declaration of Human Rights, 1948, Article 7 whereof says "All are equal before the law and are entitled without any discrimination to equal protection of the law." While ascertaining the meaning and content of these expression, however, we need not be constrained by the interpretation placed upon them in those countries though their relevance is undoubtedly great. It has to be found and determined having regard to the context and scheme of our Constitution. It appears to us that the word "law" in the former expression is used in a generic sense-a philosophical sense-whereas the word "law" in the latter expression denotes specific

laws in force.

10. Equality before law is a dynamic concept having many facets. One facet-the most commonly acknowledged-is that there shall be no privileged person or class and that none shall be above law. A facet which is of immediate relevance herein is the obligation upon the State to bring about, through the machinery of law, a more equal society envisaged by the preamble and part IV of our Constitution."

In Venkateshwara Theatre vs. State of andhra Pradesh and Others, (1993) 3 SCC 677, at paragraph Nos. 20 and 23, the Hon'ble Supreme Court, held thus:-

"20. Article 14 enjoins the State not to deny to any person equality before the law or the equal protection of the laws. The phrase "equality before the law" contains the declaration of equality of the civil rights of all persons within the territories of India. It is a basic principle of republicanism. The phrase "equal protection of laws" is adopted from the Fourteenth Amendment to U.S. Constitution. The right conferred by Article 14 postulates that all persons similarly circumstanced shall be treated alike both in privileges conferred and liabilities imposed. Since the State, in exercise of its governmental power, has, of necessity, to make laws operating differently on different groups of persons within its territory to attain particular ends in giving effect to its policies, it is recognised that the State must possess the power of distinguishing and classifying persons or things to be subjected to such laws. It is, however, required that the classification must satisfy two conditions namely, (i) it is founded on an intelligible differentia which distinguishes those that are grouped together from others; and (ii) the differentia must have a rational relation to the object sought to be achieved by the Act. It is not the requirement that the classification should be scientifically perfect or logically complete. Classification would be justified if it is not palpably arbitrary[5]. It there is equality and uniformity within each group, the law will not be condemned as discriminative, though due to some fortuitous circumstance arising out of a peculiar situation

---

5   See: Re Special Courts Bill, [1979] 2 SCR 476 at pp. 534-5361.

some included in a class get and advantage over others, so long as they are not singled out for special treatment[6].

> *23. Just a difference in treatment of persons similarly situate leads of discrimination, so also discrimination can arise if persons who are unequals, i.e. differently placed, are treated similarly. In such a case failure on the part of the legislature to classify the persons who are dissimilar in separate categories and applying the same law, irrespective of the differences, brings about the same consequence as in a case where the law makes a distinction between persons who are similarly placed. A law providing for equal treatment of unequal objects, transactions or persons would be condemned as discriminatory if there is an absence of rational relation to the object intended to be achieved by the law."*

In K. Thimmappa v. Chairman, Central Board of Directors, (2001) 2 SCC 259 that the classification under Article 14 of the Constitution of India need not be a scientifically perfect one and it is sufficient if the distinction is on just and reasonable relation to the object of the legislation. The relevant portion is as under:

"3. If the rule-making authority takes care to reasonably classify persons for a particular purpose and if it deals equally with all persons belonging to a well-defined class then it would not be open to the charge of discrimination. But to pass the test of permissible classification two conditions must be fulfilled:

(a) that the classification must be founded on an intelligible differentia which distinguishes persons or things which are grouped together from others left out of the group; and

(b) that the differentia must have a rational relation to the object sought to be achieved by the statute in question.

The classification may be founded on different basis and what is necessary is that there must be a nexus between the basis of classification and the object under consideration. Article 14 of the Constitution does not insist that the classification should be

---

6   See: Khandige Sham Bhat v. Agricultural Income-Tax Officer, [1963] 3 SCR
    809 at p. 8 171.

scientifically perfect and a court would not interfere unless the alleged classification results in apparent inequality. When a law is challenged to be discriminatory essentially on the ground that it denies equal treatment or protection, the question for determination by court is not whether it has resulted in inequality but whether there is some difference which bears a just and reasonable relation to the object of legislation. Mere differentiation does not per se amount to discrimination within the inhibition of the equal protection clause. To attract the operation of the clause it is necessary to show that the selection or differentiation is unreasonable or arbitrary; that it does not rest on any rational basis having regard to the object which the legislature has in view. If a law deals with members of a well-defined class then it is not obnoxious and it is not open to the charge of denial of equal protection on the ground that it has no application to other persons. It is for the rule-making authority to determine what categories of persons would embrace within the scope of the rule and merely because some categories which would stand on the same footing as those which are covered by the rule are left out would not render the rule or the law enacted in any manner discriminatory and violative of Article 14. It is not possible to exhaust the circumstances or criteria which may afford a reasonable basis for classification in all cases. It depends on the object of the legislation, and what it really seeks to achieve."

In Prafulla Kumar Das v. State of Orissa, (2003) 11 SCC 614, a Constitutional Bench of the Supreme Court, deciding about the validity of a legislation, held thus it would be impossible to declare a law ultra vires[7] merely because it would cause hardship, unless a case for discrimination or unreasonableness has been made out.

"In this case, the petitioners seek benefit to which they are not otherwise entitled. The legislature, in court opinion, has the requisite jurisdiction to pass an appropriate legislation which would do justice to its employees. Even otherwise a presumption to that effect has to be drawn. If a balance is sought to be struck by reason of the impugned legislation, it would not be permissible for this Court to

---

7   **Meaning of ultra vires:** Law beyond the legal power or authority of a person, corporation, agent, etc

declare it ultra vires only because it may cause some hardship to the petitioners. A mere hardship cannot be a ground for striking down a valid legislation unless it is held to be suffering from the vice of discrimination or unreasonableness. A valid piece of legislation, thus, can be struck down only if it is found to be ultra vires Article 14 of the Constitution of India and not otherwise. We do not think that in this case, Article 14 of the Constitution is attracted."

In Amita vs. Union of India, (2005) 13 SCC 721, at paragraph No. 11, the Hon'ble Supreme Court, held thus:-

"Article 14 of the Constitution of India guarantees to every citizen of India the right to equality before the law or the equal protection of law. The first expression "equality before the law" which is taken from the English common law, is a declaration of equality of all persons within the territory of India, implying thereby the absence of any special privilege in favour of any individual. It also means that amongst the equals the law should be equal and should be equally administered and that likes should be treated alike. Thus, what forbids is discrimination between persons who are substantially in similar circumstances or conditions. It does not forbid different treatment of unequal. Article 14 of the Constitution of India is both negative and positive right. Negative in the sense that no one can be discriminated against anybody and everyone should be treated as equals. The latter is the core and essence of right to equality and state has obligation to take necessary steps so that every individual is given equal respect and concern which he is entitled as a human being. Therefore, Art.14 contemplates reasonableness in the state action, the absence of which would entail the violation of Art.14 of the Constitution."

In Satyawati Sharma vs. Union of India and another, AIR 2008 SC 3148, the Hon'ble Supreme Court, observed thus:-

"Article 14 declares that the state shall not deny to any person equality before the law or the equal protection of the laws. The concept of equality embodied in Article 14 is also described as doctrine of equality. Broadly speaking, the doctrine of equality means that there should be no discrimination between one person and another, if having regard to the subject matter of legislation, their position is the same. The plain language of Article 14 may suggest that all are equal before the law and the State cannot discriminate between similarly situated persons. However, application of the doctrine of equality embodied in that Article has not been that simple. The debate which started in 1950s on the true scope of equality clause is still continuing. In last 58 years, the courts have been repeatedly called upon to adjudicate on the constitutionality of various legislative instruments including those meant for giving effect to the Directive Principals of State Policy on the ground that same violate the equality clause. It has been the constant refrain of the courts that Article 14 does not prohibit the legislature from classifying apparently similarly situated persons, things or goods into different groups provided that there is rational basis for doing so. The theory of reasonable classification has been invoked in large number of cases for repelling challenge to the constitutionality of different legislations.

1. **Discrimination in recruitment process of Sainik Schools and Rashtriya Military Schools[8]**

The Sainik Schools in its vision statement provide - To upgrade the schools as modern public schools offering education to children of common man and to effectively use technology to integrate with the futuristic knowledge-based society of emerging globalised world[9]. Whereas the admission practice institutionalizing discrimination, and in total violation of it's vision statement prohibits girls/females, while admits only Boys in Class VI of age 10-11 yrs and for Class IX of age 13-14 yrs. Sainik Schools[10], fully residential schools, affiliated

---

8   indianexpress.com/article/india/delhi-high-court-seeks-centres-reply-on-pil-for-admission-of-girls-in-sainik-schools-4993123/

9   https://www.sainikschooltvm.nic.in/ [last accessed on April 11, 2021].

10 The Sainik Schools prepare the boys academically and physically for entry into the National Defense Academy and other positions in Indian Military. Leadership qualities are cultivated through well-run house and pre-factorial systems. Students are exposed to the wholesome influence and ethos of discipline and duty so that they are brought up as sincere, dignified & well-balanced personalities as per the school motto 'Dignity and Valour'. https://www.chittorgarh.com/article/sainik-school-chittorgarh/251/ [last accessed on April 12, 2021].

34

to the CBSE, conceived in 1961 by V. K. Krishna Menon, then Defence Minister, to rectify regional and class imbalance amongst the Officer cadre of the Indian Military. Each school has extensive infrastructure & land to cater to needs of comprehensive training so that boys (only) are brought up in conducive environment[11].

Similarly, in Rashtriya Military Schools at Bangaluru, Belgaum (Karnataka) Ajmer, Dholpur (Raj) and Chail (Himachal Pradesh)[12], Admissions are exclusively for boys/ sons of Defence Service Officers and civilians. Eligible are, "Only boys between 10 to 11 years of age for Class VI and Boys between 13 to 14 years of age for class IX of age as on 01 Jul of the academic year are eligible for admission[13]. Six months relaxation in upper age limit is permissible for the wars of personnel killed in action.[14]" Admission are restricted only to boys in these schools.

The Constitution of india in Article 21A[15] guarantees free and compulsory education to all children from the age of 6 to 14 years and the consequent legislation to give effect to Article 21-A as a fundamental right is the Right of Children to Free and Compulsory Education (RTE) Act, 2009, which guarantees every child irrespective of gender a right to full time elementary education of satisfactory and equitable quality in a formal school[16].

---

11 http://www.sainikschoolsujanpurtira.org/images%5CDocuments %5C49fda1da-fcc3-486a-8e03-0e1f4157a436.pdf [last accessed on April 13, 2021].

12 https://www.rashtriyamilitaryschools.edu.in/ [last accessed on April 13, 2021].

13 https://www.rashtriyamilitaryschools.edu.in/Admission.html, [last accessed on April 13, 2021].

14 https://www.rashtriyamilitaryschools.edu.in/Admission.html, [last accessed on April 13, 2021].

15 CONSTITUTION OF INDIA, 1950, Article 21A - The State shall provide free and compulsory education to all children of the age of six to fourteen years in such manner as the State may, by law, determine.

16 RTE Act, 2009 also mandates the inclusion of 50 per cent women and parents of children from disadvantaged groups in SMCs. Such community participation will be crucial to ensuring a child friendly "whole school" environment through separate toilet facilities for girls and boys and adequate attention to health, water, sanitation and hygiene issues.

Education is one of the most critical areas of empowerment for women, and Sainik Schools and Rashtriya Military Schools, both illustrate clear examples of discrimination girls/women suffer. Offering girls basic quality education is one sure way of giving them much greater power, of enabling them to make genuine choices over the kinds of lives they wish to lead. India having ratified The Convention on the Rights of the Child[17] and the Convention on the Elimination of All Forms of Discrimination against Women[18]; and as guaranteed by Article 21 A of the Constitution of India, all establish education as a basic human right.

The deprivation of quality education by denial of admission to girls/females in Sainik Schools and Rasthtriya Military Schools is against Constitutional guarantees of Article 14,15 and 21 A, hence discriminatory.

What can be more worrying for a soldier than the education and security of his daughter/ girl child, who is deprived of quality education. Further providing quality education to a daughter of a soldier by the Indian Army is essential specially since the soldier/ father is destined to spend most of his service life away from the family in service of the nation in some operational area or the other; including running the risk of not returning. Only Sainik Schools and Rashtriya Military schools provided education in rural and semi urban areas to the wards of the Army personnel.

Article 21 of the Constitution of India has been interpreted and reinterpreted a number of times by the Supreme Court of India and its horizon has been constantly expanded keeping in view the march of times[19]. From the point of view of education, the landmark

---

17 Convention on the Rights of the Child, 1989 is an international human rights treaty which sets out the civil, political, economic, social, health and cultural rights of children

18 The Convention on the Elimination of All Forms of Discrimination against Women (CEDAW), adopted in 1979 by the UN General Assembly, is often described as an international bill of rights for women. Consisting of a preamble and 30 articles, it defines what constitutes discrimination against women and sets up an agenda for national action to end such discrimination.

19 Some of the rights that are currently included in the ambit of Article 21

decision is Constitution Bench judgment of the Supreme Court reported as *Unni Krishnan, J.P. & Ors. v. State of A.P. & Ors.,*[20] wherein the apex court held that the provisions of Parts-III and IV of the Constitution of India are supplementary and complimentary to each other and that fundamental rights are but a means to achieve the goal indicated in Part-IV, the Supreme Court held that the fundamental rights must be construed in the light of the directive principles. And because the logical corollary of the decision of the Supreme Court in the aforementioned case of Unni Krishnan case would be that free elementary education is an essential sovereign function of the welfare state because education is a cardinal component of human dignity[21].

The Preamble of the Constitution gives the direction in which the State must move i.e. to secure to all its citizens equality of status. Thus, the principle of equality is strongly expressed in the Constitution and is also in consonance with the commitments made by India by virtue of being a party to a number of international instruments.

Education is the foundation on which the society seeks to build its edifice of social harmony. It is the means through which one hopes to root out the divides that exists in society and integrate the country. Various commissions[22] have highlighted that the current multilayered school system, be it in India or abroad, promotes and maintains the wide chasm that exists between the advantaged and

---

includes: Right to live with human dignity, right to the decent environment including pollution-free water and air and protection, right to livelihood, right to privacy, right to shelter, right to health.

20 (1993) 1 SCC 645.

21 *Ibid*, para 69, 70 and 71.

22 National Education Commission (1964-1966), popularly known as Kothari Commission, was an ad hoc commission set up by the Government of India to examine all aspects of the educational sector in India, to evolve a general pattern of education and to advise guidelines and policies for the development of education in India. Also, the Secondary Education commission known as Mudaliar Commission was appointed by the government of India in term of their Resolution to bring changes in the present education system and make it better for the Nation.

disadvantaged[23]. The privilege, who can afford to buy education, have access to the high-quality elite schools, while the poor and the marginalized are left to wallow in ill-equipped schools established by the municipalities, gram panchayats and Government. Many perceive that education has become a commodity[24]. They believe that the system is inherently flawed, in that, the very means through which an egalitarian society is sought to be built is tailored in such a manner that it becomes a seat of, and a cause for, naturalising and legitimizing decisiveness and social segregation.

At present 33 Sainik Schools are operating the country[25] and government has decided to allow females/women to be admitted in sainik schools from 2021-22 but till date no admission process for girls has started in Rashtriya military schools in India even one petition regarding the same has been pending in Hon'ble Delhi High Court[26].

2. Discrimination in recruitment process of Army Educational Corps in Indian Army

At present Indian Army under its Army Educational Corps[27] entry recruits Male Candidates, *leaving no scope for employment/ recruitment for Indian Females Citizens.* By recruitment in Army Educational Corps Entry Indian Army fills up the vacancy for

---

23 Appellants: In Re: Court on its own Motion, In Re: Court on its own Motion (06.11.2015 - DELHC): MANU/DE/3407/2015.

24 Appellants: In Re: Court on its own Motion, In Re: Court on its own Motion (06.11.2015 - DELHC): MANU/DE/3407/2015.

25 https://www.hindustantimes.com/education/admissions/govt-decides-to-admit-girl-cadets-in-all-sainik-schools-from-202122-101615436186165.html [last accessed on April 15, 2021].

26 https://www.thehindu.com/news/cities/Delhi/hc-acts-on-pil-over-sainik-schools/article22234054.ece [last accessed on April 16, 2021].

27 Their work is to teach different subjects like Economics/History/Geography/ Pol Science/Philosophy/Psychology/Sociology/Public Administration/ Statistics/International Relation/International Studies etc. Only those candidates who have passed Post Graduate Degree MA/M.Sc in the following subjects /M.Com/MCA/MBA with 1st or 2nd Division can apply for Army Educational Corps.

English, Geography, Economics, History, Geology, Botany, Physics, Chemistry etc. Teachers[28].

This discrimination on the grounds of gender is violative of fundamental right of equality before Law[29], Right not to be discriminated on the ground of sex[30], equality of opportunity in the matters of public employment[31], fundamental right to practice any profession and occupation and human rights of the women[32].

High Court of Kerala in A.N. Rajamma vs. State of Kerala and Ors.[33], held that the *State shall not discriminate against any citizen on grounds only of sex is one of the most important fundamental rules that calls for strict observance.* In para 34 of the judgment court observed that:

"The mandate to the State that it shall not discriminate against any citizen on grounds only of sex is one of the most important fundamental rules that calls for strict observance. In the framing of any statute or law or the making of subordinate legislation by a delegated legislative authority this is a fundamental rule which, under no circumstances, would bear violation. Unlike the freedoms in Article 19 of the Constitution there is no Scope for restricting the absolute scope of the rights under Article 15(1) of the Constitution. There would be no scope whatever to justify differentiating between the male and female sexes in the matter of appointment. The right of women should not be denied on fanciful assumptions of what work the woman could do and could not do. Whether the work is of an arduous nature and therefore unsuitable for women must be decided from the point of view of how women feel about it and how they would assess it. If the work of say, a Duffadar, a Cleaner-cum-Conductor, Court Keeper, Chairman, Housekeeper or a Field Worker

28 http://www.joinindianarmy.nic.in/writereaddata/Portal/NotificationPDF/DETAILED_NOTIFICATION_AEC_122.pdf [last accessed on April 15, 2021].

29 CONSTITUTION OF INDIA, 1950, Article 14.

30 CONSTITUTION OF INDIA, 1950. Article 15.

31 CONSTITUTION OF INDIA, 1950, Article 16.

32 CONSTITUTION OF INDIA, 1950, Article 19(1)(g).

33 MANU/KE/0139/1983.

does not suit a woman or she would feel humiliated by such work it is for her to decide whether she should apply for the concerned job and not for the male dominated legislature or the male dominated bureaucratic machinery which may be functioning as a delegated legislative body to decide whether women should be permitted to do such work or not."

In Vasantha R. v. Union of India and Ors.[34], high court observed that woman is no longer content merely to sit at home expecting the man to earn the bread for the family and await him for his return. Both are quite often equal partners in sharing the financial burden of running the home. This social change must necessarily have its impact upon traditional perspectives concerning woman's role and that must call for change in our laws and such laws should be to advance the constitutional guarantees and such laws and provisions shall not be affront to the rights guaranteed by Articles 14, 15, 16 and 19 of the Constitution as the Constitution mandates equality. No rule should operate as a deterrent to such change, but such a rule should advance or promote equality. Perhaps the time has come where all posts should be thrown open to men and women equally-except those which due to physical reasons women cannot take up.

There is no purpose/justification for the eligibility criteria regarding recruitment of only male candidates to Army Educational Corps and excluding female candidates, meaning thereby that Indian Army is treating equals un-equally. This condition by Indian Army to recruit only male citizens is arbitrary and discriminatory against women.

3. **Discrimination in recruitment process of 10+2 Technical Entry Scheme Course (Permanent Commission) and University Entry Scheme (Permanent Commission)**

Recruitment only of Unmarried male candidates to the 10+2 Technical Entry Scheme Course (Permanent Commission) and University Entry Scheme (Permanent Commission) by Indian Army[35], violates Article 14 of the Indian Constitution. As per this

---

34 MANU/TN/0549/2000.

35 https://joinindianarmy.nic.in/writereaddata/Portal/NotificationPDF/TES_45. pdf [last accessed on April 15, 2021].

article, the State shall not deny to any person equality before law or the equal protection of laws within the territory of India. Article 15(1) of the Indian Constitution provides that "the State shall not discriminate against any citizen on grounds only of religion, race, caste, sex, place of birth or any of them" and article 16, article 19 (1) (g) and Article 39 A in Part IV of the Constitution deals with Directive Principles of State Policy which provides that the State shall direct its policies towards securing that the citizens, men and women equally, have the right to adequate means of livelihood.

The State might be having some rational or basis for not recruiting females in Army but that classification has to stand the test of "reasonable basis for treating equals differently" as laid down by the Hon'ble Supreme Court in the matter of *Air India Etc. v. Nergesh Meerza & Ors.*[36], which is reproduced as below:

"(2) Art. 14 forbids hostile discrimination but not reason able classification. Thus, where persons belonging to a particular class in view of their special attributes, qualities, mode of recruitment and the like, are differently treated in public interest to advance and boost members belonging to backward classes, such a classification would not amount to discrimination having a close nexus with the objects sought to be achieved so that in such cases Art. 14 will be completely out of the way. (3) Art. 14 certainly applies where equals are treated differently without any reasonable basis."

"(6) In order to judge whether a separate category has been carved out of a class of service, the following circumstances have generally to be examined:-

(a) the nature, the mode and the manner of recruitment of a particular category from the very start,

(b) the classifications of the particular category.

(c) the terms and conditions of service of the members of the category,

(d) the nature and character of the posts and promotional avenues,

---

36 1981 AIR 1829, 1982 SCR (1) 438.

(e) the special attributes that the particular category possess which are not to be found in other classes, and the like."

As per the test listed above the recruitment process of 10 + 2 Technical Entry Scheme Course (Permanent Commission) and University Entry Scheme (Permanent Commission) violates article 14 of Indian Constitution.

In M/s. Dwarka Prasad Laxmi Naraian v. The State of Uttar Pradesh & Ors. Court made the following observations:-

"Legislation, which arbitrarily or excessively invades the right, cannot be said to contain the quality of reasonableness, and unless it strikes a proper balance between the freedom guaranteed under article 19 (1) (g) and the social control permitted by clause (6) of article 19, it must be held to be wanting in reasonableness."

Equality is a dynamic concept with many aspects and dimensions and it cannot be imprisoned within traditional and doctrinaire limits. Article 14 strikes at arbitrariness in State action and ensures fairness and equality of treatment. The principle of reasonableness, which legally as well as philosophically, is an essential element of equality or non-arbitrariness pervades Article 14 like a brooding omnipresence. It must be "right and just and fair" and not arbitrary, fanciful or oppressive[37]; otherwise, it would be no procedure at all and the requirement of Article 21 would not be satisfied.

The present condition of recruitment to 10 + 2 Technical Entry Scheme Course (Permanent Commission) and University Entry Scheme (Permanent Commission) of Indian ends up victimizing its subject (women). In that regard the interference prescribed by state for pursuing the ends of protection should be proportionate to the legitimate aims. The standard for judging the proportionality should be a standard capable of being called reasonable in a modern democratic society[38]. Instead of putting curbs on women's freedom,

---

37 Maneka Gandhi v. Union of India (UOI) and Ors. (25.01.1978 - SC) : MANU/SC/0133/1978.

38 State of Maharashtra and Ors. v. Indian Hotel and Restaurants Assn. and Ors. (16.07.2013 - SC): MANU/SC/0702/2013.

empowerment would be a more tenable and socially wise approach. This empowerment should reflect in the law enforcement strategies of the state as well as law modelling done in this behalf.

4. Discrimination in recruitment process of Indian Navy[39]

At present, Recruiting Branch of Indian Navy recruits only males and not females as Sailors, Steward, Cook and Topass for serving in the Indian Navy. Due to this institutionalized discrimination, female candidates who are qualified as per the advertisements published by Indian Navy for the post of Sailors, Steward, Cook and Topass are being deprived of their right to serve in Indian Navy as Sailors, Steward, Cook and Topass[40]. This discrimination on grounds of gender is violative of fundamental right of equality before Law[41], Right not to be discriminated on the ground of sex[42], equality of opportunity in the matters of public employment[43], fundamental right to practice any profession and occupation and human rights of the women[44].

The role of Cook is to prepare food as per menu (both vegetarian and non-vegetarian including of meat products) and accounting of ration. The role of Steward is to serve the food in the officers' messes, as waiters, housekeeping, accounting of funds, wine and stores, preparation of menu. The role of Topasses is to work as safaiwalas, including cleaning of toilets.

Presently male candidates are recruited by recruitment department of Indian Navy which violates the Constitutional Principles. To prevent discrimination against women on the grounds of marriage/gender,

---

39 https://govt-jobs.euttaranchal.com/wp-content/uploads/2019/11/Cook-Steward-Sweeper-Recruitment-in-Indian-Navy.pdf [last accessed on April 16, 2021].

40 https://www.joinindiannavy.gov.in/files/event_attachments/ 1512125694_529781.pdf [last accessed on Apri 17, 2021].

41 CONSTITUTION OF INDIA, 1950, Article 14.

42 CONSTITUTION OF INDIA, 1950, Article 15.

43 CONSTITUTION OF INDIA, 1950, Article 16.

44 CONSTITUTION OF INDIA, 1950, Article 19(1)(g).

it requires States/parties to take appropriate measures to prohibit dismissal on the grounds of pregnancy/gender and discrimination in dismissals on the basis of marital status/gender. It also requires the introduction of maternity leave with pay or with comparable social benefits without loss of former employment, seniority or social allowance.

Further Indian Navy practices institutional discrimination, without any rationale basis arbitrarily deprive FEMALES the right to serve in the Indian Navy University Entry Scheme, Executive Branch General Service (X) Cadre, IT, and in TECHNICAL BRANCH Engineering and Electrical Branch, while permitting entry as Air Traffic Controller and Naval Architecture. Discrimination on grounds of gender is violative of the fundamental right of equality (Art 14), Right not to be discriminated on the ground of sex (Art 15), equality of opportunity in the matters of public employment (Art 16), fundamental right to practice any profession and occupation (Art 19 1 (g)) and human rights of the women.

There is no rational or basis for not permitting entry of female candidates in the Indian Navy University Entry Scheme, Executive Branch General Service (X) Cadre, IT, and in technical branch, Engineering and Electrical Branch at par with Males; nor does such discrimination stand the test of "reasonable basis for treating equals differently".

The subordination of one sex to the other ought to be replaced by a principle of perfect equality, admitting no power or privilege on the one side, nor disability on the other.[45] Denial of appointment to women to posts on the sole ground that they are women is opposed to Articles 14 and 15(1) of the Constitution, excepting in those fields where either women are totally unsuitable or they do not come forward or for physical reasons women cannot take up particular kind of job or jobs.

Today the Indian Air Force (IAF) today, having completed the Platinum Jubilee of dedicated service to the nation, is a modern, technology-intensive force distinguished by its commitment to

---

45 Hon'ble Court in Kush Kalra v. UOI, WP (C) 10498/2015

excellence and professionalism. Keeping pace with the demands of contemporary advancements, the IAF continues to modernise in a phased manner and today it stands as a credible air power counted amongst the fore-most professional services in the world.

The primacy of Air Power will be a decisive factor in shaping the outcome of future conflicts. There is no reasonable justification for depriving inclusion of women/females as Airmen in group "X" trade and group "Y" trade in all the departments of Air Force by the Indian Air Force. On one hand the Indian Air Force makes claims in the Indian Air force about joining of women as pilots and making history[46]. Whereas the fact is that the Indian Air force instead of being benevolent employer for women, is indulging in discriminatory practices against women without any reasonable justification for post of Airmen in group "X" trade and group "Y" trade in all the departments of Indian Air Force.

---

46 https://www.ndtv.com/india-news/three-women-pilots-of-indian-air-force-iaf-set-to-fly-frontline-military-jets-1759178.

Chapter - 5

Equality for Women

India is a welfare State and, therefore, it is the duty of the State to promote justice, to provide equal opportunity to all citizens and see that they are not deprived of by reasons of economic disparity. It is also the duty of the State to frame policies so that men and women have the right to adequate means of livelihood. It is also the duty of the citizen to strive towards excellence in all spheres of individual and collective activity so that the nation constantly rises to higher levels of endeavour and achievement.

All forms or dimensions of discrimination on ground of gender is violative of fundamental freedom and human rights. The Convention for elimination of all forms of discrimination against women was ratified by the United Nations Organisation on December 18, 1979 and the Government of India had ratified as an active participant on June 19, 1993. It has been reiterated that the discrimination against women violates the principle of equality, of rights as well as respect for human dignity. Article 1 of the Convention for Elimination of all forms of Discrimination Against Women (CEDAW) defines the expression "Discrimination Against Women" to mean "any distinction, exclusion or restriction made on the basis of sex which has the effect or purpose of impairing or nullifying the recognised enjoyment or exercise by women, irrespective of their marital status, on the basis of equality of men and women, all human rights and fundamental freedoms in the political, economic, social, cultural, civil or any other field.

In the matter of *National Legal Services Authority v. Union of India*, (2014) 5 SCC 438 the Supreme Court recognized that gender identity, is an integral part of sex within the meaning of Articles 15 and 16 of the Constitution of India and no citizen can be discriminated on the ground of gender.

In *Royappa Vs. State of Tamil Nadu and Anr.*, AIR1974SC555 Court held that:

"Article 16 embodies the fundamental guarantee that there shall be equality of opportunity for all citizens in matters relating to employment or appointment to any office under the State. Though enacted as a distinct and independent fundamental right because of its great importance as a principle ensuring equality of opportunity in public employment which is so vital to the building up of the new classless egalitarian society envisaged in the Constitution, Article 16 is only an instance of the application of the concept of equality enshrined in Article 14. In other words, Article 14 is the genus while Article 16 is a species, Article 16 gives effect to the doctrine or equality in all matters relating to public employment. The basic principle which, therefore, informs both Articles 14 and 16 is equality and inhibition against discrimination."……….

"The basic principle which, therefore, informs both Articles 14 and 16 is equality and inhibition against discrimination. Now, what is the content and reach of this great equalising principle? It is a founding faith, to use the words of Bose, J., "a way of life", and it must not be subjected to a narrow pedantic or lexicographic approach. We cannot countenance any attempt to truncate its all-embracing scope and meaning, for to do so would be to violate its activist magnitude. Equality is a dynamic concept with many aspects and dimensions and it cannot be "cribbed, cabined and confined" within traditional and doctrinaire limits. From a positivistic point of view, equality is antithetic to arbitrariness. In fact equality and arbitrariness are sworn enemies; one belongs to the rule of law in a republic while the other, to the whim and caprice of an absolute monarch. Where an act is arbitrary it is implicit in it that it is unequal both according to political logic and Constitutional law and is therefore violative of Article 14, and if it affects any matter relating to public employment, it is also violative of Article 16. Articles 14 and 16 strike at arbitrariness in State action and ensure fairness and equality of treatment. They require that State action must be based on equivalent relevant principles applicable alike to all similarly situate and it must not be guided by any extraneous or irrelevant considerations because that would be denial of equality."

As regards the ascendancy of women in the sphere of public employment, the Apex Court has observed that when a discrimination is sought to be made on the purported ground of classification, such classification must be founded on rational criteria. The criteria in the absence of any constitutional provision and, it will bear repetition to state, having regard to the societal conditions as they prevailed in early 20th century, may not be a rational criteria in the 21st century. In the early 20th century, the hospitality sector was not open to women in general. In the last 60 years, women in India have gained entry in all spheres of public life. They have also been representing people at grassroots democracy. They are now employed as drivers of heavy transport vehicles, conductors of service carriages, police etc. Women can be seen to be occupying Class IV posts to the post of a Chief Executive Officer of a multinational company. They are now widely accepted both in the Police as also Army services.

The State might be having some rational or basis for not recruiting females in Army but that classification has to stand the test of "reasonable basis for treating equals differently" as laid diown by the Hon'ble Supreme Court in the matter of **"Air India Etc. Vs Nergesh Meerza & Ors.**: 1981 AIR 1829, 1982 SCR (1) 438, which is reproduced as below:

> *"(2) Art. 14 forbids hostile discrimination but not reason able classification. Thus, where persons belonging to a particular class in view of their special attributes, qualities, mode of recruitment and the like, are differently treated in public interest to advance and boost members belonging to backward classes, such a classification would not amount to discrimination having a close nexus with the objects sought to be achieved so that in such cases Art. 14 will be completely out of the way. (3) Art. 14 certainly applies where equals are treated differently without any reasonable basis."*

"(6) In order to judge whether a separate category has been carved out of a class of service, the following circumstances have generally to be examined:-

(a) the nature, the mode and the manner of recruitment of a particular category from the very start,

(b) the classifications of the particular category.

(c) the terms and conditions of service of the members of the category,

(d) the nature and character of the posts and promotional avenues,

(e) the special attributes that the particular category possess which are not to be found in other classes, and the like."

In M/s. Dwarka Prasad Laxmi Naraian v. The State of Uttar Pradesh & Ors. ....this Court made the following observations:-

"Legislation, which arbitrarily or excessively invades the right, cannot be said to contain the quality of reasonableness, and unless it strikes a proper balance between the freedom guaranteed under article 19 (1) (g) and the social control permitted by clause (6) of article 19, it must be held to be wanting in reasonableness."

In Maneka Gandhi v. Union of India,.............. Beg, C.J. Observed as follows:

"The view I have taken above proceeds on the assumption that there are inherent or natural human rights of the individual recognised by and embodied in our Constitution.. If either the reason sanctioned by the law is absent, or the procedure followed in arriving at the conclusion that such a reason exists is unreasonable, the order having the effect of deprivation or restriction must be quashed."

and Bhagwati, J. Observed thus:

"Equality is a dynamic concept with many aspects and dimensions and it cannot be imprisoned within traditional and doctrinaire limits. Article 14 strikes at arbitrariness in

State action and ensures fairness and equality of treatment. The principle of reasonableness, which legally as well as philosophically, is an essential element of equality or non-arbitrariness pervades Article 14 like a brooding omnipresence. It must be "right and just and fair" and not arbitrary, fanciful or oppressive; otherwise, it would be no procedure at all and the requirement of Article 21 would not be satisfied."

CEDAW to which India is also a signatory in article 1 states "*Article I*

For the purposes of the present Convention, the term "discrimination against women" shall mean any distinction, exclusion or restriction made on the basis of sex which has the effect or purpose of impairing or nullifying the recognition, enjoyment or exercise by women, irrespective of their marital status, on a basis of equality of men and women, of human rights and fundamental freedoms in the political, economic, social, cultural, civil or any other field."

In the erstwhile Soviet Union after the Second World War what was considered to be physically impossible for women in India was being performed by women in U.S.S.R. including loading and unloading of wheat bags each weighing 100 kilograms or thereabout in flour mills or rail heads or as well as in transit sheds. At any rate, every effort should be taken to advance equality and there shall be no discrimination on the ground of sex. Denial of appointment to women to posts on the sole ground that they are women is opposed to Articles 14 and 15(1) of the Constitution, excepting in those fields where either women are totally unsuitable or they do not come forward or for physical reasons women cannot take up particular kind of job or jobs.[1]

---

1 *Vasantha R. v. Union of India and Ors.,* MANU/TN/0549/2000 **(2001) IILLJ 843 Mad**

Role of Indian Judiciary in Promoting Gender Equality

Case-1

Gender equality is one of the basic principles of our Constitution[2]

Facts in Nutshell:

The first petitioner[3] the wife of the second petitioner. The first petitioner, a writer and several of her books are said to have been published by Penguin. The second petitioner, a Medical Scientist in Jawaharlal Nehru University, New Delhi. They jointly applied to the Reserve Bank of India (first respondent[4]) on 10.12.1984 for 9% Relief Bonds in the name of their minor son Rishab Bailey for Rs. 20,000/-. They stated expressly that both of them agreed that the mother of the child, i.e., the first petitioner would act as the guardian[5] of the minor[6] for the purpose of investments made with

---

2 Appellants: **Ms. Githa Hariharan & Anr. Vs.** Respondent: **Reserve Bank of India & Anr.** AIR1999SC1149 **Hon'ble Judges/Coram:** Dr. A. S. Anand, CJI., M. Srinivasan and U. C. Banerjee, JJ.

3 **Meaning of Petitioner:** A person who presents a Petition. (**Meaning of Petition:** A formal message requesting something that is submitted to an authority)

4 **Meaning of Respondent:** A **respondent** is a person who is called upon to issue a response to a communication made by another. In legal usage, this specifically refers to the defendant in a legal proceeding commenced by a petition, or to an appellee, or the opposing party, in an appeal of a decision by an initial fact-finder

5 A **legal guardian** is a person who has the legal authority (and the corresponding duty) to care for the personal and property interests of another person, called a ward. Usually, a person has the status of guardian because the ward is incapable of caring for his or her own interests due to infancy, incapacity, or disability. Most countries and states have laws that provide that the parents of a minor child are the legal guardians of that child, and that the parents can designate who shall become the child's legal guardian in the event of death, subject to the approval of the court. Courts generally have the power to appoint a guardian for an individual in need of special protection

6 In law, a *minor* is a person under a certain age—usually the age of majority—which legally demarcates childhood from adulthood. The age of majority depends upon jurisdiction and application, but is generally 18. *Minor* may also

the money held by their minor son. Accordingly, in the prescribed form of application, the first petitioner signed as the guardian of the minor. The first respondent replied to the petitioners advising them either to produce the application form signed by the father of the minor or a certificate of guardianship from a competent authority in favour of the mother. That lead to the filing of writ petition[7] by the two petitioners with prayers to strike down Section 6(a)[8] of the Hindu Minority and Guardianship Act, 1956, (hereinafter referred to as HMG Act) and Section 19(b)[9] of the Guardian and

---

be used in contexts unconnected to the overall age of majority. For example, the drinking age in the United States is 21, and people below this age are sometimes called *minors* even if they are older than 18.

7 **Meaning of Writ Petition:** Under the Indian legal system, jurisdiction to issue 'prerogative writs' is given to the Supreme Court, and to the High Courts of Judicature of all Indian states. Parts of the law relating to writs are set forth in the Constitution of India. The Supreme Court, the highest in the country, may issue writs under Article 32 of the Constitution for enforcement of Fundamental Rights and under Articles 139 for enforcement of rights other than Fundamental Rights, while High Courts, the superior courts of the States, may issue writs under Articles 226. 'Writ' is eminently designed by the makers of the Constitution, and in the same way it is developed very widely and efficiently by the courts in India. The Constitution broadly provides for five kinds of "prerogative" writs, namely, Habeas Corpus, Certiorari, Mandamus, Quo Warranto and Prohibition

8 *Section 6(a) of the Hindu Minority and Guardianship Act, 1956*
   Natural guardians of a Hindu minor.-
   The natural guardians of a Hindu, minor, in respect of the minor's person as well as in respect of the minor's property (excluding his or her undivided interest in joint family property), are -
   (a) in the case of a boy or an unmarried girl—the father, and after him, the mother: provided that the custody of a minor who has not completed the age of five years shall ordinarily be with the mother;
   (b) in the case of an illegitimate boy or an illegitimate unmarried girl - the mother, and after her, the father;
   (c) in the case of a married girl – the husband;
   Provided that no person shall be entitled to act as the natural guardian of a minor under the provisions of this section—
   (a) if he has ceased to be a Hindu, or
   (b) if he has completely and finally renounced the world by becoming a hermit (vanaprastha) or an ascetic (yati or sanyasi)

9 **Section 19 in The Guardians And Wards Act, 1890**

Wards Act, 1890 (hereinafter referred to as GW Act) as violative of Articles14[10] & 15[11] of the Constitution and to quash and set aside the decision of the first respondent refusing to accept the deposit from the petitioners and to issue a mandamus[12] directing the acceptance

---

Guardian not to be appointed by the Court in certain cases.- Nothing in this Chapter shall authorize the Court to appoint or declare a guardian of the property of a minor whose property is under the superintendence of a Court of Wards, or to appoint or declare a guardian of the person--

(a) of a minor who is a married female and whose husband is not, in the opinion of the Court, unfit to be guardian of her person, or

(b) of a minor whose father is living and is not, in the opinion of the Court, unfit to be guardian of the person of the minor, or

(c) of a minor whose property is under the superintendence of a Court of Wards competent to appoint a guardian of the person of the minor.

10 **Article 14 in The Constitution Of India 1949**
Equality before law: The State shall not deny to any person equality before the law or the equal protection of the laws within the territory of India Prohibition of discrimination on grounds of religion, race, caste, sex or place of birth

11 **Article 15 in The Constitution Of India 1949**
15. Prohibition of discrimination on grounds of religion, race, caste, sex or place of birth

(1) The State shall not discriminate against any citizen on grounds only of religion, race, caste, sex, place of birth or any of them

(2) No citizen shall, on grounds only of religion, race, caste, sex, place of birth or any of them, be subject to any disability, liability, restriction or condition with regard to

(a) access to shops, public restaurants, hotels and palaces of public entertainment; or

(b) the use of wells, tanks, bathing ghats, roads and places of public resort maintained wholly or partly out of State funds or dedicated to the use of the general public

(3) Nothing in this article shall prevent the State from making any special provision for women and children

(4) Nothing in this article or in clause (2) of Article 29 shall prevent the State from making any special provision for the advancement of any socially and educationally backward classes of citizens or for the Scheduled Castes and the Scheduled Tribes

12 **Mandamus** is a judicial remedy in the form of an order from a superior court, to any government subordinate court, corporation, or public authority—to do (or forbear from doing) some specific act which that body is obliged under law to do (or refrain from doing)—and which is in the nature of public duty, and in certain cases one of a statutory duty. It cannot be issued to compel an authority

of the same after declaring the first petitioner as the natural guardian of the minor.

Hindu Minority and Guardianship Act, 1956:

The HMG Act came into force in 1956, i.e., six years after the Constitution. Did the Parliament intend to transgress[13] the constitutional limits or ignore the fundamental rights[14] guaranteed by the Constitution which essentially prohibits discrimination on grounds of sex? In Courts opinion - No. It is well settled that if on one construction a given statute will become unconstitutional, whereas on another construction, which may be open, the statute remains within the constitutional limits, the Court will prefer the latter on the ground that the Legislature is presumed to have acted in accordance with the Constitution and courts generally lean in favour of the constitutionality of the statutory provisions.

Section 6 of the HMG Act reads as follows:

The natural guardians of a Hindu minor, in respect of the minor's person as well as in respect of the minor's property (excluding his or her undivided interest in joint family property), are-

(a) in the case of a boy or an unmarried girl - the father, and after him, the mother provided that the custody of a minor who has not completed the age of five years shall ordinarily be with the mother;

---

to do something against statutory provision. For example, it cannot be used to force a lower court to reject or authorize applications that have been made, but if the court refuses to rule one way or the other then a mandamus can be used to order the court to rule on the applications.

13 **Meaning of Transgress:**
1. To break (a law, rule, etc)
2. to go beyond or overstep (a limit)

14 **Meaning of Fundamental Rights:** The Fundamental Rights are defined as basic human freedoms which every Indian citizen has the right to enjoy for a proper and harmonious development of personality. These rights universally apply to all citizens, irrespective of race, place of birth, religion, caste, creed, colour or gender. Aliens (persons who are not citizens) are also considered in matters like equality before law. They are enforceable by the courts, subject to certain restrictions.

(b) in the case of an illegitimate boy or an illegitimate unmarried girl - the mother, and after her, the father;

(c) in the case of a married girl - the husband;

Provided that no person shall be entitled to act as the natural guardian of a minor under the provisions of this section-

(a) if he has ceased to be a Hindu, or (b) if he has completely and finally renounced the world becoming a hermit (vanaprastha) or an ascetic (yati or sanyasi).

Explanation-1 In this section, the expression "father" and "mother" do not include a step-father and a step-mother".

The expression 'natural guardian' is defined in Section 4(c) of HMG Act as any of the guardians mentioned in Section 6 (supra). The term 'guardian' is defined in Section 4(b) of HMG Act as a person having the care of the person of a minor or of his property or of both, his person and property, and includes a natural guardian among others. Thus, it is seen that the definitions of 'guardian' and 'natural guardian' do not make any discrimination against mother and she being one of the guardians mentioned in Section 6 would undoubtedly be a natural guardian as defined in Section 4(c). The only provision to which exception is taken is found in Section 6(a)which reads "the father, and after him, the mother", (underlining ours). That phrase, on a cursory reading, does give an impression that the mother can be considered to be natural guardian of the minor only after the lifetime of the father. In fact that appears to be the basis of the stand taken by the Reserve Bank of India also. It is not in dispute and is otherwise well settled also that welfare of the minor in the widest sense is the paramount consideration and even during the life time of the father, if necessary, he can be replaced by the mother or any other suitable person by an order of court, where to do so would be in the interest of the welfare of the minor.

Issue in Dispute:

In the present case, the Reserve Bank of India has questioned the authority of the mother, even when she had acted with the concurrence of the father, because in its opinion (Bank Opinion) she could function as a guardian only after the life time of the father and not during his life time.

Decision by Supreme Court:

Court held that while both the parents are duty bound to take care of the person and property of their minor child and act in the best interest of his welfare, Court hold that in all situations where the father is not in actual charge of the affairs of the minor either because of his indifference or because of an agreement between him and the mother of the minor (oral or written) and the minor is in the exclusive care and custody of the mother or the father for any other reason is unable to take care of the minor because of his physical and/or mental incapacity, the mother, can act as natural guardian of the minor and all her actions would be valid even during the life time of the father, who would be deemed to be 'absent' for the purposes of Section 6(a) of HMG Act and Section19(b) of GW Act.

Hence, the Reserve Bank of India was not right in insisting upon an application signed by the father or an order of the Court in order to open a deposit account[15] in the name of the minor particularly when there was already a letter jointly written by both petitioners evidencing their mutual agreement.

---

15 A deposit account is a savings account, current account, or other type of bank account, at a banking institution that allows money to be deposited and withdrawn by the account holder.

Case-2

Government cannot deny maternity leave for birth of a third Child[16]

Facts in Nutshell

Petitioner[17]/Appellant[18] – **Ruksana**, who was appointed as a Multipurpose Health Worker (Female) on 18.7.2007 in the State of Haryana, by way writ petition[19] approached the High Court and

---

16 Appellants: Ruksana Vs. Respondent: State of Haryana and Ors.
Subject: Maternity Benefit Act, 1961
Hon'ble Judges/Coram: Ranjan Gogoi, C.J. and Kanwaljit Singh Ahluwalia, Judge, High Court of Punjab and Haryana at Chandigarh (2012)166PLR106, 2011(2)SCT789(P&H)

17 **Meaning of petitioner:**
a. A formal written application seeking a court's intervention and action on a matter
b. A pleading initiating a legal case in some civil courts

18 **Meaning of Appellant:**
One who appeals a court decision.

19 **Writ Petition**
A petition seeking issuance of a writ is a writ petition. Pits in the first instance in the High Courts and the Supreme Court are writ petitions. A writ of habeas corpus is issued to an authority or person to produce in court a person who is either missing or kept in illegal custody. Where the detention is found to be without authority of law, the Court may order compensation to the person illegally detained. A writ of mandamus is a direction to an authority to either do or refrain from doing a particular act. For instance, a writ to the Pollution Control Board to strictly enforce the Pollution Control Acts. For a mandamus to be issued, it must be shown:
a) That the authority was under obligation, statutory or otherwise to act in a particular manner;
b) that the said authority failed in performing such obligation;
c) that such failure has resulted in some specific violation of a fundamental right of either the petitioner or an indeterminate class of persons.
A writ of certiorari is a direction to an authority to produce before the Court the records on the basis of which a decision under challenge in the writ petition has been taken. By looking into those records, the Court will examine whether the authority applied its mind to the relevant materials before it took the decision. If the Court finds that no reasonable person

questioned the validity of Note 4 to Rule 8.127 of the Punjab Civil Services Rules Volume I Part I so far it restricts grant of benefit of maternity leave to the birth of two living children. In the writ petition, it has been prayed that by issuing writ[20] in the nature of certiorari[21] Note 4 to the above said Rules be quashed[22] being ultra vires[23] to the Constitution of India and contrary to the mandatory dictum[24] of law laid in the Maternity Benefit Act, 1961 (hereinafter referred to as "the Act"). Not only the vires of the Note in question appended

---

could come to the decision in question, it will set aside (quash) that decision and give a further direction to the authority to consider the matter afresh. For instance, the permission given by an authority to operate a distillery next to a school can be challenged by filing a petition asking for a writ of certiorari. A writ of prohibition issues to prevent a judicial authority subordinate to the High Court from exercising jurisdiction over a matter pending before it. This could be on the ground that the authority lacks jurisdiction and further that prejudice would be caused if the authority proceeds to decide the matter. Where the authority is found to be biased and refuses to rescue, a writ of prohibition may issue. A petition seeking a writ of quo warranto questions the legal basis and authority of a person appointed to public office. For instance, the appointment of a member of a Public Service Commission not qualified to hold the post can be questioned by a writ of quo warranto and appointment nullified if found to be illegal.

20 **Meaning of writ:**
A written order issued by a court, commanding the party to whom it is addressed to perform or cease performing a specified act.

21 **Certiorari** is a writ seeking judicial review. It is issued by a superior court, directing an inferior court, tribunal, or other public authority to send the record of a proceeding for review.

22 **Meaning of quash:**
To annul or put an end to (a court order, indictment, or court proceedings).

23 **Ultra vires** is a Latin phrase meaning "beyond the powers". If an act requires legal authority and it is done with such authority, it is characterised in law as **intra vires** ("within the powers"). If it is done without such authority, it is *ultra vires*. Acts that are *intra vires* may equivalently be termed "valid" and those that are *ultra vires* "invalid".

24 **Meaning of dictum:**
A side remark made in a judicial opinion that is not necessary for the decision in the case and therefore is not to be regarded as establishing the law of the case or setting legal precedent. Also called *obiter dictum*.

to Rule have been assailed[25] being contrary to the Maternity Benefit Act, 1961 but it has also been urged that the Note cannot sustain in the eyes of law being contrary to right of equality, guaranteed under Articles 14[26] and 16[27] of the Constitution of India as it suffers from the vice of discrimination. Along with the above said two thrust arguments, Executive Instructions issued by the Government of Haryana which bring to an end the distinction of two living children born before or after entering into the service have also been challenged. Petitioner/Appellant, who has conceived a child as a first one from the second marriage has also contended that the child to be born first from the second marriage, cannot be construed as third child to deny benefit of maternity leave.

---

25 **Meaning of assail:**

   1. To attack violently, as with blows or military force; assault.

   2. To attack verbally, as with ridicule or censure.

26 **Article 14 in The Constitution Of India 1949**

   14. Equality before law The State shall not deny to any person equality before the law or the equal protection of the laws within the territory of India Prohibition of discrimination on grounds of religion, race, caste, sex or place of birth

27 **Article 16 in The Constitution Of India 1949**

   16. Equality of opportunity in matters of public employment

   (1) There shall be equality of opportunity for all citizens in matters relating to employment or appointment to any office under the State

   (2) No citizen shall, on grounds only of religion, race, caste, sex, descent, place of birth, residence or any of them, be ineligible for, or discriminated against in respect or, any employment or office under the State

   (3) Nothing in this article shall prevent Parliament from making any law prescribing, in regard to a class or classes of employment or appointment to an office under the Government of, or any local or other authority within, a State or Union territory, any requirement as to residence within that State or Union territory prior to such employment or appointment

   (4) Nothing in this article shall prevent the State from making any provision for the reservation of appointments or posts in favor of any backward class of citizens which, in the opinion of the State, is not adequately represented in the services under the State

   (5) Nothing in this article shall affect the operation of any law which provides that the incumbent of an office in connection with the affairs of any religious or denominational institution or any member of the governing body thereof shall be a person professing a particular religion or belonging to a particular denomination

Brief Facts:

The Petitioner/Appellant was appointed as a Multipurpose Health Worker (female) on the recommendation of the Haryana Staff Selection Commission, Panchkula vide appointment letter dated 18.7.2007. Before joining the Government service, the Petitioner/ Appellant was married to one Farukh Ali and two children were born from the wedlock, who were earlier staying with the Petitioner/ Appellant. According to Petitioner/Appellant, marriage has been dissolved on 13.1.2010 by way of decree[28] of divorce granted by the District Judge, Family Court, Faridabad and thereafter custody of the children was with their father. Vide order dated 9.2.2011 passed by High Court, the decree of divorce granted to the Petitioner attained finality. After the decree of divorce was granted by the Court the Petitioner/Appellant has solemnized marriage with one Mukim Khan. It was stated that from the second marriage, the Petitioner/ Appellant was expecting a child in March 2011. The Petitioner/ Appellant had applied for grant of maternity leave. On 16.2.2011, the Respondent[29]- **State of Haryana and Ors.** denied maternity leave to the Petitioner/Appellant on the ground that she was already having two living children.

Chapter VIII of Punjab Civil Services Rules Volume I Part-I defines "Maternity Leave" and the same reads as under:

8.127(1) The competent authority under Rule 8.23 may grant maternity leave to a female Government employee for a period not exceeding three months from the date of its commencement or to the end of six weeks from the date of confinement whichever is earlier. Leave salary equal to the pay drawn immediately before proceeding on leave shall be paid during maternity leave and it shall not be debited against the leave account. Controversy in this case revolves around Note 4 appended to this Rule and the same reads as under: -

---

28 **Meaning of decree:**
   a. The judgment of a court of equity.
   b. The judgment of a court.

29 **Meaning of Respondent:**
   The defending party in certain legal proceedings, as in a case brought by petition.

Note 4 Maternity leave shall not be admissible to a female Government employee having more than two living children. In such cases leave of the kind due or extra ordinary leave will be allowed.

The Respondents had issued Executive Instructions to clarify the above said Note and on the basis thereof maternity leave had been denied. The said Executive Instructions issued on 5.2.1993 read as under:-

Whether a female Govt. employee can avail of the benefit of maternity leave when she has already two living children before joining the Govt. service. The matter has been considered by the Govt. and it was accordingly, clarified that a female Govt. employee who has already two living children before her entry into Govt. service, is not entitled to the benefit of maternity leave. In such cases the deptts. may consider granting leave of the kind due to the female employees.

As per this clarification, the benefit of maternity leave was to be restricted to the two living children.

Contentions by the learned counsel for the Appellant:

Learned Counsel for the Petitioner/Appellant contended that the act of the employer to deny maternity leave to an employee having more than two living children was arbitrary and cause discrimination between two sets of women i.e. one who is having two living children and another who is having more than two children. It was stated that such a classification is not permissible in law and is violative of the principles of equality, enshrined in Articles 14 and 16 of the Constitution of India. Secondly, it was contended that to give effect to the Directive Principles of State Policy[30] especially Article

---

30 The **Directive Principles of State Policy** are guidelines or principles given to the central and state governments of India, to be kept in mind while framing laws and policies. These provisions, contained in Part IV of the Constitution of India, are not enforceable by any court, but the principles laid down therein are considered fundamental in the governance of the country, making it the duty of the State[1] to apply these principles in making laws to establish a just society in the country. The principles have been inspired by the Directive Principles given in the Constitution of Ireland relate to social justice, economic welfare, foreign policy, and legal and administrative matters.

42[31] of the Constitution of India which expects the State to make provisions for securing just and humane condition of work and for grant of maternity leave, the Central Government has enacted the Maternity Act, 1961 which is Socio Beneficial Act and the provisions of the Maternity Act, 1961 shall override all the Rules framed by the Government. It was urged that the Rules framed by the Respondent-Government ought to be in consonance with the Act and so far as the Rules overstep the statutory provisions of the Act, they are to be quashed being in derogation to the Central Statute.

Lastly, it is argued that since the child conceived and expected to be born was the first child from the second marriage, denial of maternity leave to the Petitioner/Appellant will defeat the very purpose for which the Maternity Act was enacted. It was urged that the Maternity Act, 1961 intended to empower women to take employment, to supplement income of the family and be equal partner in the marriage. Pregnancy, delivery and rearing of child should not confine women to home and therefore to strengthen the institution of marriage benefit of maternity leave was thought over.

Contention by the learned counsel for the Respondent:

It was contended by the learned counsel that Section 28[32] of the

---

31 Article 42 in The Constitution Of India 1949
  42. Provision for just and humane conditions of work and maternity relief: The State shall make provision for securing just and humane conditions of work and for maternity relief.

32 **Section 28 in The Maternity Benefit Act, 1961**

28. Power to make rules.—
  (1) The appropriate Government may, subject to the condition of previous publication and by notification in the Official Gazette, make rules for carrying out the purposes of this Act.
  (2) In particular, and without prejudice to the generality of the foregoing power, such rules may provide for—

  (a) the preparation and maintenance of registers, records and muster-rolls;
  (b) the exercise of powers (including the inspection of establishments) and the performance of duties by Inspectors for the purposes of this Act;
  (c) the method of payment of maternity benefit and other benefits under this Act in so far as provision has not been made therefor in this Act;

Maternity Act, 1961 empowers the Government to make Rules in carrying out the purposes of the Act therefore, under Clause (k) of Sub Section (2) to Section 28 of the Act, the Government can make Rules or in respect of any other matter, which is to be, or may be prescribed pertaining to maternity benefit. It was stated that under the Rule making power which vests in the Government under Section 28 of the Maternity Act, 1961 necessary provisions were incorporated in the Punjab Civil Services Rules as applicable to the State of Haryana with regard to the maternity and hospital leave. *It was further stated that Rules do not make distinction between the first and second marriage and the benefits of the maternity leave were restricted only to two living children.*

Questions before the High Court:

i) Whether the classification of women employees, one having two children and another having more than two children was just and

---

(d) the form of notices under section 6;

(e) the nature of proof required under the provisions of this Act;

(f) the duration of nursing breaks referred to in section 11;

(g) acts which may constitute gross misconduct for purposes of section 12;

(h) the authority to which an appeal under clause (b) of sub-section (2) of section 12 shall lie; the form and manner in which such appeal may be made and the procedure to be followed in disposal thereof;

(i) the authority to which an appeal shall lie against the decision of the Inspector under section 17; the form and manner in which such appeal may be made and the procedure to be followed in disposal thereof;

(j) the form and manner in which complaints may be made to Inspectors under sub-section (1) of section 17 and the procedure to be followed by them when making inquiries or causing inquiries to be made under sub-section (2) of that section;

(k) any other matter which is to be, or may be, prescribed.

[(3) Every rule made by the Central Government under this section shall be laid as soon as may be after it is made, before each House of Parliament while it is in session for a total period of thirty days which may be comprised in one session 1[or in two or more successive sessions and if, before the expiry of the session immediately following the session or the successive sessions, aforesaid] both Houses agree in making any modification in the rule or both Houses agree that the rule should not be made, the rule shall thereafter have effect only in such modified form or be of no effect, as the case may be; so, however, that any such modification or annulment shall be without prejudice to the validity of anything previously done under that rule.

appropriate? Whether the Government can create such a distinction?

ii) Whether having two children from the previous marriage will eclipse the right of a woman to obtain maternity benefit for the first child to be born from the second marriage?

Reasonable classification:

Classification between the women having two children or more was considered by the Hon'ble Apex Court in *Javed and Ors. v. State of Haryana and Ors.*[33] . The vires of the provisions of Sections 175(1)(q) and 177(1) of the Haryana Panchayati Raj Act, 1994, were questioned before the Hon'ble Apex Court. By these provisions, persons having two living children were disqualified to hold the office of the Sarpanch or a Panch of the Gram Panchayat. Such a classification was assailed being ultra vires to the Constitution of India. It was canvassed[34] that the provision was arbitrary and hence violative of Article 14 of the Constitution of India and was also discriminatory. In Javeds case, it was held that even though Article 14 of the Constitution of India forbids class legislation, it does not forbid reasonable classification for the purposes of legislation. Thus, classification between two sets of women employees having two children or more than two was held to be reasonable.

Decision by the High Court:

Court was of the view that State was well justified in making a distinction between the two sets of women employees, one having two living children and another having more than two living children. Such a classification being reasonable was having intelligible differentia to achieve the object of family planning.

Family planning is a part of National Public Policy and the State

---

33 (2003) 8 SCC 369

34 **Meaning of canvass:**
   1. An examination or discussion.
   2. A solicitation of votes or orders.
   3. A survey of public opinion.

to achieve this object can grant incentives and also put restrictions upon the benefits which have to flow to the employees. Therefore, as per court the classification of women employees, one having two children and another having more than two children was just and appropriate by the respondent--state.

The Maternity Act, 1961 as per Section 2[35], applies to all the establishments of the Government. Section 27 of the Maternity Act, 1961 specifically states that there is no fetter on the Rule making power of the organization so long as it is more beneficial to an employee than the one envisaged in the Act. However, all rules which are inconsistent with the provisions of the Act shall not eclipse the provisions of the Act. Section 27 of the Act reads as under:

27. Effect of laws and agreements inconsistent with this Act. (1) The provisions of this Act shall have effect notwithstanding anything inconsistent therewith contained in any other law or in the terms of any award, agreement or contract of service, whether made before or after the coming into force of this Act:

Provided that where under any such award, agreement, contract of

---

35 Section 2 in The Maternity Benefit Act, 1961

2. Application of Act.—

(1) It applies, in the first instance,—

(a) to every establishment being a factory, mine or plantation including any such establishment belonging to Government and to every establishment wherein persons are employed for the exhibition of equestrian, acrobatic and other performances;

(b) to every shop or establishment within the meaning of any law for the time being in force in relation to shops and establishments in a State, in which ten or more persons are employed, or were employed, on any day of the preceding twelve months:] Provided that the State Government may, with the approval of the Central Government, after giving not less than two month's notice of its intention of so doing, by notification in the Official Gazette, declare that all or any of the provisions of this Act shall apply also to any other establishment or class of establishments, industrial, commercial, agricultural or otherwise.

(2) [Save as otherwise provided in [sections 5A and 5B] nothing contained in this Act] shall apply to any factory or other establishment to which the provisions of the Employees' State Insurance Act, 1948 (34 of 1948), apply for the time being.

service or otherwise, a woman is entitled to benefits in respect of any matter which are more favourable to her than those to which she would be entitled under this Act, the woman shall continue to be entitled to the more favourable benefits in respect of that matter, notwithstanding that she is entitled to receive benefit in respect of other matters under this Act.

(2) Nothing contained in this Act shall be construed to preclude a woman from entering into an agreement with her employer for granting her rights or privileges in respect of any matter, which are more favourable to her than those to which she would be entitled under this Act.

The Act nowhere restricts the benefit of payment of maternity benefits to birth of two children. In other words, the provisions of the Act entitle the woman employee to maternity benefits for the birth of third child too.

Court was conscious that by Note 4 to Rule 8.127 of the Punjab Civil Services Rules Volume I Part I, the State Government intended to achieve a laudable object but such an object cannot be given effect to till the establishments of the Government are amenable to the Act. Unless an amendment was carried out in the Maternity Act, 1961 the Government cannot restrict beneficial provisions of the Maternity Act, 1961 to a woman employee for the birth of a third child. Such a restriction imposed under the Rules was contrary to Section 27 of the Maternity Act, 1961 and cannot sustain in the eyes of law.

Thus, court was of the opinion that Note 4 to Rule 8.127 of the Punjab Civil Services Rules Volume I Part I was not in consonance with the provisions of the Maternity Act,1961 and this cannot be given effect to and the Petitioner/Appellant cannot be deprived of the maternity benefit for the birth of a third child.

Court held that the Petitioner-employee was entitled to the payment of salary as maternity leave benefit as envisaged under Section 5[36] of

---

36 Section 5 in The Maternity Benefit Act, 1961
    5. Right to payment of maternity benefits.—

the Maternity Act, 1961 read with Rule 8.127 of the Punjab Civil Services Rules Volume I Part I.

---

(1) Subject to the provisions of this Act, every woman shall be entitled to, and her employer shall be liable for, the payment of maternity benefit at the rate of the average daily wage for the period of her actual absence, that is to say, the period immediately preceding the day of her delivery, the actual day of her delivery and any period immediately following that day.] Explanation.— For the purpose of this sub-section, the average daily wage means the average of the woman's wages payable to her for the days on which she has worked during the period of three calendar months immediately preceding the date from which she absents herself on account of maternity, 1[the minimum rate of wage fixed or revised under the Minimum Wages Act, 1948 (11 of 1948) or ten rupees, whichever is the highest].

(2) No woman shall be entitled to maternity benefit unless she has actually worked in an establishment of the employer from whom she claims maternity benefit, for a period of not less than [eighty days] in the twelve months immediately preceding the date of her expected delivery: Provided that the qualifying period of [eighty days] aforesaid shall not apply to a woman who has immigrated into the State of Assam and was pregnant at the time of the immigration. Explanation.—For the purpose of calculating under the sub-section the days on which a woman has actually worked in the establishment 3[the days for which she has been laid off or was on holidays declared under any law for the time being in force to be holidays with wages] during the period of twelve months immediately preceding the date of her expected delivery shall be taken into account.

(3) The maximum period for which any woman shall be entitled to maternity benefit shall be twelve weeks of which not more than six weeks shall precede the date of her expected delivery:] Provided that where a woman dies during this period, the maternity benefit shall be payable only for the days up to and including the day of her death: [Provided further that where a woman, having been delivered of a child, dies during her delivery or during the period immediately following the date of her delivery for which she is entitled for the maternity benefit, leaving behind in either case the child, the employer shall be liable for the maternity benefit for that entire period but if the child also dies during the said period, then, for the days up to and including the date of the death of the child.

Case-3

Unwed mothers don't need father's consent for guardianship of child[37]

Facts in Nutshell:

Appeal[38] was filed by appellant[39] -- **ABC** against the judgment dated 8.8.2011 delivered by the High Court of **Delhi**, which has dismissed the First Appeal of the Appellant, who is an unwed mother, holding that her guardianship application cannot be entertained unless she discloses the name and address of the father of her child, thereby enabling the Court to issue process to him. The Appellant, who adheres to the Christian faith, is well educated, gainfully employed and financially secure. She gave birth to her son in 2010, and has subsequently raised him without any assistance from or involvement of his putative father. Desirous of making her son her nominee in all her savings and other insurance policies, she took steps in this direction, but was informed that she must either declare the name of the father or get a guardianship/adoption certificate from the Court. She thereupon filed an application Under Section 7[40] of the

37 Appellants: **ABC Vs.** Respondent: **The State (NCT of Delhi)**
   Hon'ble Judges/Coram:
   Vikramajit Sen and Abhay Manohar Sapre, JJ., Supreme court of India
   MANU/SC/0718/2015, Decided On: 06.07.2015
   Subject: Family Law

38 **Meaning of Appeal:**
   a. A higher court's review of the correctness of a decision by a lower court.
   b. A case so reviewed.
   c. A request for a higher court to review the decision of a lower court.

39 **Meaning of Appellant:**
   One who appeals a court decision.

40 **Section 7 in The Guardians and Wards Act, 1890**
   7. Power of the Court to make order as to guardianship.—
   (1) Where the Court is satisfied that it is for the welfare of a minor that an order should be made—
   (a) appointing a guardian of his person or property or both, or
   (b) declaring a person to be such a guardian the Court may make an order accordingly.
   (2) An order under this section shall imply the removal of any guardian who has not been appointed by will or other instrument or appointed or declared by

Guardians and Wards Act, 1890 (the Act) before the Guardian Court for declaring her the sole guardian of her son. Section 11[41] of the Act requires a notice to be sent to the parents of the child before a guardian is appointed. The Appellant published a notice of the petition[42] in a daily newspaper, but was strongly averse to naming the father. She filed an affidavit[43] stating that if at any time in the future the father

the Court.

(3) Where a guardian has been appointed by will or other instru ment or appointed or declared by the Court, an order under this section appointing or declaring another person to be guardian in his stead shall not be made until the powers of the guardian appointed or declared as aforesaid have ceased under the provisions of this Act.

41 11. Procedure on admission of application
(1) If the Court is satisfied that there is ground for proceeding on the application, it shall fix a day for the hearing thereof, and cause notice of the application and of the date fixed for the hearing-
(a) to be served in the manner directed in the Code of Civil Procedure,1882(14 of 1882)11 on-
(i) the parents of the minor if they are residing in 11 [any State to which this Act extends;]
(ii) the person, if any, named in the petition or letter as having the custody or possession of the person or property of the minor;
(iii) the person proposed in the application or letter to be appointed or declared guardian, unless that person is himself the applicant; and
(iv) any other person to whom, in the opinion of the court special notice of the applicant should be given; and
(b) to be posted on some conspicuous part of the court-house and of the residence of the minor, and otherwise published in such manner as the court, subject to any rules made by the High Court under this Act, thinks fit.
(2) The State Government may, by general or special order, require that when any part of the property described in a petition under section 10, sub-section (1), is land of which a Court of Wards could assume the superintendence, the court shall also cause a notice as aforesaid to be served on the Collector in whose district the minor ordinarily resides and on every Collector in whose district any portion of the land is situate, and the Collector may cause the notice to be published in any manner he deems fit.
(3) No charge shall be made by the court or the Collector for the service or publication of any notice served or published under sub-section (2).

42 **Meaning of Petition:**
A formal written application seeking a court's intervention and action on a matter

43 **Meaning of Affidavit:**

of her son raises any objections regarding his guardianship, the same may be revoked or altered as the situation may require.

Decision by Guardian Court:

The Guardian Court directed her to reveal the name and whereabouts of the father and consequent to her refusal to do so, dismissed her guardianship application on 19.4.2011.

Decision by High Court:

The Appellant's appeal before the High Court was dismissed on the reasoning that her allegation that she is a single mother could only be decided after notice is issued to the father; that a natural father could have an interest in the welfare and custody of his child even if there is no marriage; and that no case can be decided in the absence of a necessary party.

Question before the Supreme Court:

 Whether it is imperative for an unwed mother to specifically notify the putative father of the child whom she has given birth to of her petition for appointment as the guardian of her child.

The Guardians and Wards Act, 1890

The Act, which applies to Christians in India, lays down the procedure by which guardians are to be appointed by the Jurisdictional Court. Sections 7, 11 and 19 are as follows:

7. Power of the court to make order as to guardianship

(1) Where the court is satisfied that it is for the welfare of a minor that an order should be made-

(a) appointing a guardian of his person or property, or both,

Or

(b) declaring a person to be such a guardian,

the court may make an order accordingly.

A written declaration made under oath before a notary public or other authorized officer.

(2) An order under this section shall imply the removal of any guardian who has not been appointed by will or other instrument or appointed or declared by the court.

(3) Where a guardian has been appointed by will or other instrument or appointed or declared by the court, an order under this section appointing or declaring another person to be guardian in his stead shall not be made until the powers of the guardian appointed or declared as aforesaid have ceased under the provisions of this Act.

The details of the form of application are contained in Section 10 and the procedure that applies to a guardianship application is prescribed in Section 11.

11. Procedure on admission of application

(1) If the Court is satisfied that there is ground for proceeding on the application, it shall fix a day for the hearing thereof, and cause notice of the application and of the date fixed for the hearing-

(a) to be served in the manner directed in the Code of Civil Procedure, 1882 (14 of 1882)11 on-

(i) the parents of the minor if they are residing in any **State** to which this Act extends;

(ii) the person, if any, named in the petition or letter as having the custody or possession of the person or property of the minor;

(iii) the person proposed in the application or letter to be appointed or declared guardian, unless that person is himself the applicant; and

(iv) any other person to whom, in the opinion of the court special notice of the applicant should be given; and

(b) to be posted on some conspicuous part of the court-house and of the residence of the minor, and otherwise published in such manner as the court, subject to any rules made by the High Court under this Act, thinks fit.

(2) The **State** Government may, by general or special order, require that when any part of the property described in a petition Under Section 10, Sub-section (1), is land of which a Court of Wards could

assume the superintendence, the court shall also cause a notice as aforesaid to be served on the Collector in whose district the minor ordinarily resides and on every Collector in whose district any portion of the land is situate, and the Collector may cause the notice to be published in any manner he deems fit.

(3) No charge shall be made by the court or the Collector for the service or publication of any notice served or published Under Sub-section (2).

Section 19 is of significance, even though the infant son does not independently own or possess any property, in that it specifically alludes to the father of a minor. It reads thus:

19. Guardian not to be appointed by the court in certain cases

Nothing in this Chapter shall authorise the court to appoint or declare a guardian of the property of a minor whose property is under the superintendence of a Court of Wards or to appoint or declare a guardian of the person-

(a) of a minor who is a married female and whose husband is not, in the opinion of court, unfit to be guardian of her person; or

(b) of a minor whose father is living and is not in the opinion of the court, unfit to be guardian of the person of the minor; or

(c) of a minor whose property is under the superintendence of a Court of Wards competent to appoint a guardian of the person of the minor.

Guardianship as dealt under different statutes in India:

Section 6(b) of the Hindu Minority and Guardianship Act, 1956 makes specific provisions with respect to natural guardians of illegitimate children, and in this regard gives primacy to the mother over the father. Mohammedan law accords the custody of illegitimate children to the mother and her relations. The law follows the principle that the maternity of a child is established in the woman who gives birth to it, irrespective of the lawfulness of her connection with the begetter[44].

---

44 **Meaning of begetter:**

However, paternity is inherently nebulous[45] especially where the child is not an offspring of marriage. Furthermore, as per Section 8 of the Indian Succession Act, 1925, which applies to Christians in India, the domicile of origin of an illegitimate child is in the country in which at the time of his birth his mother is domiciled. This indicates that priority, preference and pre-eminence is given to the mother over the father of the concerned child.

Guardianship law around the world:

In the United Kingdom, the Children Act 1989 allocates parental responsibility, which includes all rights, duties, powers, responsibilities and authority of a parent over the child and his/her property. According to Section 2(2) of that Act, parental custody of a child born of unwed parents is with the mother in all cases, and additionally with the father provided he has acquired responsibility in accordance with the provisions of the Act. To acquire responsibility, he would have to register as the child's father, execute a parental responsibility agreement with the mother or obtain a Court order giving him parental responsibility over the child.

In the U.S.A., each **State** has different child custody laws but predominantly the mother has full legal and physical custody from the time the child is born. Unless an unmarried father establishes his paternity over the child it is generally difficult for him to defeat or overwhelm the preferential claims of the mother to the custody. However, some **States** assume that both parents who sign the child's Birth Certificate have joint custody, regardless of whether they are married.

In Ireland, Section 6(4) of the Guardianship of Infants Act, 1964 ordains-"The mother of an illegitimate infant shall be guardian of

---

1. (especially of a male parent) to procreate or generate (offspring).

2. to cause; produce as an effect

45 **Meaning of nebulous:**
1. hazy, vague, indistinct, or
a nebulous recollection of the meeting; a nebulous distinction between pride and conceit.
2. cloudy or cloud like.

the infant." Unless the mother agrees to sign a statutory declaration, an unmarried father must apply to the Court in order to become a legal guardian of his child. Article 176 of the Family Code of the Philippines explicitly provides that "illegitimate children shall use the surname and shall be under the parental authority of their mother, and shall be entitled to support in conformity with this Code." This position obtains regardless of whether the father admits paternity. In 2004, the Supreme Court of the Philippines in *Joey D. Briones v. Maricel P. Miguel* et al, G.R. No. 156343, held that an illegitimate child is under the sole parental authority of the mother.

The law in New Zealand, as laid out in Section 17 of the Care of Children Act, 2004, is that the mother of a child is the sole guardian if she is not married to, or in civil union with, or living as a de facto partner with the father of the child at any time during the period beginning with the conception of the child and ending with the birth of the child.

In South Africa, according to the Children's Act No. 38 of 2005, parental responsibility includes the responsibility and the right (a) to care for the child; (b) to maintain contact with the child; (c) to act as guardian of the child; and (d) to contribute to the maintenance of the child. The biological mother of a child, whether married or unmarried, has full parental responsibilities and rights in respect of the child. The father has full parental responsibility if he is married to the mother, or if he was married to her at the time of the child's conception, or at the time of the child's birth or any time in between, or if at the time of the child's birth he was living with the mother in a permanent life-partnership, or if he (i) consents to be identified or successfully applies in terms of Section 26 to be identified as the child's father or pays damages in terms of customary law; (ii) contributes or has attempted in good faith to contribute to the child's upbringing for a reasonable period; and (iii) contributes or has attempted in good faith to contribute towards expenses in connection with the maintenance of the child for a reasonable period. This conspectus[46] indicates that the preponderant[47] position that it is the unwed mother who possesses primary custodial and guardianship rights with regard to her children and that the father is not conferred with an equal position merely by virtue of his having fathered the child.

It is thus abundantly clear that the predominant legal thought in different civil and common law jurisdictions spanning the globe as well as in different statutes within India is to bestow guardianship and related rights to the mother of a child born outside of wedlock. Avowedly[48], the mother is best suited to care for her offspring, so aptly and comprehensively conveyed in Hindi by the word 'mamta'. Furthermore, recognizing her maternity would obviate[49] the necessity of determining paternity. In situations where the father has not exhibited any concern for his offspring, giving him legal recognition would be an exercise in futility. In today's society, where women are increasingly choosing to raise their children alone, and a man who has chosen to forsake his duties and responsibilities is not a necessary constituent for the wellbeing of the child.

Cases in which welfare of the child was given paramount[50] concern:

In Laxmi Kant Pandey v. Union of India51 1985, Supreme Court prohibited notice of guardianship applications from being issued to the biological parents of a child in order to prevent them from

---

46 **Meaning of conspectus:**
    1. a general or comprehensive view; survey.
    2. a digest; summary; résumé.

47 **Meaning of Preponderant:**
    Superior in weight, force, influence, numbers, etc

48 **Meaning of Avowed**: Acknowldged, Decalred

49 **Meaning of obviate:**
    To anticipate and prevent or eliminate (difficulties, disadvantages, etc.) by effective measures; render unnecessary:

50 Meaning of Paramount:
    chief in importance or impact; supreme

51 (Supp) SCC 701

tracing the adoptive parents and the child. Although the Guardians and Wards Act was not directly attracted in that case, nevertheless it is important as it reiterates that the welfare of the child takes priority above all else, including the rights of the parents.

In *Githa Hariharan v. Reserve Bank of India*[52] where the RBI[53] had refused to accept an application for a fixed deposit in the name of the child signed solely by the mother. In the context of Section 6 of the Hindu Minority and Guardianship Act as well as Section 19 of the Guardians and Wards Act, Supreme Court had clarified that "in all situations where the father is not in actual charge of the affairs of the minor either because of his indifference or because of an agreement between him and the mother of the minor (oral or written) and the minor is in the exclusive care and custody of the mother or the father for any other reason is unable to take care of the minor because of his physical and/or mental incapacity, the mother can act as natural guardian of the minor and all her actions would be valid even during the life time of the father who would be deemed to be "absent" for the purposes of Section 6(a)[54] of the HMG Act and

---

52 (1999) 2 SCC 228

53 The **Reserve Bank of India** is India's central banking institution, which controls the monetary policy of the Indian rupee. It commenced its operations on 1 April 1935 during the British Rule in accordance with the provisions of the Reserve Bank of India Act, 1934. The original share capital was divided into shares of 100 each fully paid, which were initially owned entirely by private shareholders. Following India's independence on 15 August 1947, the RBI was nationalised on 1 January 1949.

54 *6.Natural guardians of a Hindu minor.-*
The natural guardians of a Hindu, minor, in respect of the minor's person as well as in respect of the minor's property (excluding his or her undivided interest in joint family property), are –
(a) in the case of a boy or an unmarried girl—the father, and after him, the mother: provided that the custody of a minor who has not completed the age of five years shall ordinarily be with the mother;
(b) in the case of an illegitimate boy or an illegitimate unmarried girl – the mother, and after her, the father;
(c) in the case of a married girl – the husband;
Provided that no person shall be entitled to act as the natural guardian of a minor under the provisions of this section—
(a) if he has ceased to be a Hindu, or

Section 19(b)[55] of the GW Act." Supreme Court has construed the word 'after' in Section 6(a) of the Hindu Minority and Guardianship Act as meaning "in the absence of-be it temporary or otherwise or total apathy of the father towards the child or even inability of the father by reason of ailment or otherwise." Thus Supreme Court interpreted the legislation before it in a manner conducive[56] to granting the mother, who was the only involved parent, guardianship rights over the child.

Convention on the Rights of the Child:

The Convention on the Rights of the Child, which India has acceded to on 11th November, 1992. This Convention pointedly makes mention, inter alia[57], to the Universal Declaration of Human Rights. For facility of reference the salient provisions are reproduced-

Article 1

For the purposes of the present Convention, a child means every human being below the age of eighteen years unless under the law applicable to the child, majority is attained earlier.

Article 3

(b) if he has completely and finally renounced the world by becoming a hermit (vanaprastha) or an ascetic (yati or sanyasi)
Explanation.—In this section, the expressions 'father' and 'mother' do not include a step-father and a step-mother.

55 **19. Guardian not to be appointed by the court in certain cases**
Nothing in this Chapter shall authorise the court to appoint or declare a guardian of the property of a minor whose property is under the superintendence of a Court of Wards or to appoint or declare a guardian of the person-
(a) of a minor who is married female and whose husband is not, in the opinion of court, unfit to be guardian of her person; or
(b) 15[* * *] of a minor whose father is living and is not in the opinion of the court, unfit to be guardian of the person of the minor; or
(c) of a minor whose property is under the superintendence of a Court of Wards competent to appoint a guardian of the person of the minor.

56 **Meaning of Conducive:**
Tending to produce; contributive; helpful; favorable

57 Meaning of Inter-Alia:
Among other things

1. In all actions concerning children, whether undertaken by public or private social welfare institutions, courts of law, administrative authorities or legislative bodies, the best interests of the child shall be a primary consideration.

2. **States** Parties undertake to ensure the child such protection and care as is necessary for his or her well-being, taking into account the rights and duties of his or her parents, legal guardians, or other individuals legally responsible for him or her, and, to this end, shall take all appropriate legislative and administrative measures.

3. **States** Parties shall ensure that the institutions, services and facilities responsible for the care or protection of children shall conform with the standards established by competent authorities, particularly in the areas of safety, health, in the number and suitability of their staff, as well as competent supervision.

Article 7

1. The child shall be registered immediately after birth and shall have the right from birth to a name, the right to acquire a nationality and, as far as possible, the right to know and be cared for by his or her parents.

Article 9

1. **States** Parties shall ensure that a child shall not be separated from his or her parents against their will, except when competent authorities subject to judicial review determine, in accordance with applicable law and procedures, that such separation is necessary for the best interests of the child. Such determination may be necessary in a particular case such as one involving abuse or neglect of the child by the parents, or one where the parents are living separately and a decision must be made as to the child's place of residence.

2. In any proceedings pursuant to paragraph 1 of the present article, all interested parties shall be given an opportunity to participate in the proceedings and make their views known.

3. **States** Parties shall respect the right of the child who is separated

from one or both parents to maintain personal relations and direct contact with both parents on a regular basis, except if it is contrary to the child's best interests.

Article 12

1. **States** Parties shall assure to the child who is capable of forming his or her own views the right to express those views freely in all matters affecting the child, the views of the child being given due weight in accordance with the age and maturity of the child.

2. For this purpose, the child shall in particular be provided the opportunity to be heard in any judicial and administrative proceedings affecting the child, either directly, or through a representative or an appropriate body, in a manner consistent with the procedural rules of national law.

Article 18

1. **States** Parties shall use their best efforts to ensure recognition of the principle that both parents have common responsibilities for the upbringing and development of the child. Parents or, as the case may be, legal guardians, have the primary responsibility for the upbringing and development of the child. The best interests of the child will be their basic concern.

Article 21

States Parties that recognize and/or permit the system of adoption shall ensure that the best interests of the child shall be the paramount consideration and they shall:

(a) Ensure that the adoption of a child is authorized only by competent authorities who determine, in accordance with applicable law and procedures and on the basis of all pertinent and reliable information, that the adoption is permissible in view of the child's status concerning parents, relatives and legal guardians and that, if required, the persons concerned have given their informed consent to the adoption on the basis of such counselling as may be necessary;

Article 27

2. The parent(s) or others responsible for the child have the primary responsibility to secure, within their abilities and financial capacities, the conditions of living necessary for the child's development.

4. **States** Parties shall take all appropriate measures to secure the recovery of maintenance for the child from the parents or other persons having financial responsibility for the child, both within the **State**Party and from abroad. In particular, where the person having financial responsibility for the child lives in a **State** different from that of the child, **States** Parties shall promote the accession to international agreements or the conclusion of such agreements, as well as the making of other appropriate arrangements.

Decision by Supreme Court:

Court directed that if a single parent/unwed mother applies for the issuance of a Birth Certificate for a child born from her womb, the Authorities concerned may only require her to furnish an affidavit[58] to this effect, and must thereupon issue the Birth Certificate, unless there is a Court direction to the contrary. Supreme Court emphasized that it is the responsibility of the **State** to ensure that no citizen suffers any inconvenience or disadvantage merely because the parents fail or neglect to register the birth. Nay[59], it is the duty of the **State** to take requisite steps for recording every birth of every citizen.

Supreme Court directed the Guardian Courts to recall the dismissal order passed by it and thereafter consider the Appellant's application for guardianship expeditiously[60] without requiring notice to be given to the putative father of the child.

---

58 **Meaning of Affidavit:**
A written declaration upon oath made before an authorized official.

59 **Meaning of Nay:**
And not only so but; not only that but also; indeed

60 **Meaning of expeditiously:**
Characterized by promptness; quick

Case-4

Moms of Surrogate Babbies can get maternity leave[61]

Facts in Nutshell:

A synthesis of science and divinity (at least for those who believe in it), led to the culmination of the petitioner's[62]/appellant[63]-- **Rama Pandey**desire for a child. Married, on 18.01.1998, to one Sh. Atul Pandey, the petitioner's, wish to have a child was fulfilled on 09.02.2013, albeit[64] via the surrogacy[65] route. Her bundle of joy comprised of twins, who were born on the aforementioned date, at a city hospital.

To effectuate the aforesaid purpose, the petitioner had entered into an arrangement with, one, Ms. Aarti, wife of Mr. Surya Narayan (hereafter referred to as the **surrogate** mother). The arrangement required the **surrogate** mother to bear a child by employing the In-Vitro Fertilization (IVF) methodology[66]. The methodology used and agreed upon required the genetic father to fertilize, In-Vitro, the

---

61 Appellants: **Rama Pandey Vs.** Respondent: **Union of India and Ors.**

Hon'ble Judges/Coram:**Rajiv Shakdher**, Judge, High Court of Delhi

Subject: Service Law

MANU/DE/2054/**2015**, Decided On: 17.07.**2015**

62 **Meaning of Petitioner:**
A person who presents a petition

63 **Meaning of Appellant:**
One who appeals a court decision.

64 **Meaning of Albeit:**
Even though; although; notwithstanding

65 **Meaning of surrogacy:**
The state of being a surrogate or surrogate mother.

66 *In vitro* **fertilization** or **fertilization** (IVF) is a process by which an egg is fertilised by sperm outside the body: *in vitro* ("in glass"). The process involves monitoring and stimulating a woman's ovulatory process, removing an ovum or ova (egg or eggs) from the woman's ovaries and letting sperm fertilise them in a liquid in a laboratory. The fertilised egg (zygote) is cultured for 2–6 days in a growth medium and is then implanted in the same or another woman's uterus, with the intention of establishing a successful pregnancy.

ovum supplied by a designated donor. The resultant embryo was then required to be transferred and implanted in the **surrogate** mother. This arrangement, along with other terms and conditions, which included rights and obligations of the commissioning parents, as also those of the **surrogate** mother, were reduced to a written agreement dated 08.08.2012 (in short the surrogacy agreement).

The fact that the surrogacy agreement reached fruition, is exemplified by the birth of twins on 09.02.2013. This far, the petitioner was happy; her unhappiness, however, commenced with rejection of her application dated 06.06.2013, for grant of maternity and Child Care Leave (CCL).

By her application before High Court, the petitioner/appellant sought 180 days maternity leave and 3 months CCL as respondents no.3[67]--Kendriya Vidyalaya Sangathan (KVS) have not considered petitioner's request.

It was conveyed to the petitioner by respondent No.3 that there was no provision for grant of maternity leave in cases where the surrogacy route is adopted. The petitioner was, however, informed that the CCL could be sanctioned, in her favour, under Rule 43-A, which was applicable to "female government servants".

Submission by Petitioner/Appellant Counsel:

The counsel for the petitioner equated the position of a commissioning mother to that of a biological mother who bears and carries the child till delivery. It was the submission of the learned counsel for the petitioner, that the commissioning parents have a huge emotional interest in the well-being of both the **surrogate** mother and the child, which the **surrogate** mother carries, albeit under a contractual arrangement. The well-being of the child and the **surrogate** mother can best be addressed by the commissioning parents, in particular, the commissioning mother. This object, according to the learned counsel, can only be effectuated, if maternity leave is granted to the

---

67 **Meaning of respondent:**
    The defending party in certain legal proceedings, as in a case brought by petition.adj.

commissioning mother.

New Reproductive Technologies (NRT):

With the advent of New Reproductive Technologies (NRT) or what are also known as Assisted Reproductive Technologies (ART), (after the birth of the first test-tube baby Louise Joy Brown, in 1978), there has been a veritable explosion of possibilities for achieving and bringing to term a pregnancy. It appears that in future one would have three kinds of mothers:

(i) a genetic mother, who donates or sells her eggs;

(ii) a **surrogate** or natal mother, who carries the baby; and

(iii) a social mother, who raises the child[68].

India's first test-tube baby Kanupriya alias Durga, brought to fore the use of similar technology in India. The reproduction of children by NRTs or ARTs, raises several moral, legal and ethical issues. Though the science proceeded in this direction in the late 1970, the practice of having children via surrogacy is, a more recent phenomena.

Maternity Leave Rules:

The relevant leave rules were first framed in 1972; to which amendments have been made from time to time. While notions have changed vis-a-vis[69] parenthood, there appears to be an inertia in recognising that motherhood can be attained even via surrogacy.

Rule 43 implicitly recognises that there are two principal reasons why maternity leave is accorded. First, that with pregnancy, biological changes occur. Second, post childbirth "multiple burdens" follow. (See : C-366/99 Griesmar, [2001] ECR 1-9383)

Therefore, if one were to recognise even the latter reason the

---

68 See: Feminist Perspectives on Law, Chapter 4: Facilitating Motherhood, pages 121-123.

69 **Meaning of Vis-a-vis:**

1. Face to face with; opposite to.

2. Compared with.

3. In relation to.

commissioning mother, to my mind, ought to be entitled to maternity leave.

It is clearly foreseeable that a commissioning mother needs to bond with the child and at times take over the role of a breast-feeding mother, immediately after the delivery of the child.

In sum, the commissioning mother would become the principal care giver upon the birth of child; notwithstanding the fact that child in a given situation is bottle-fed.

It follows thus, that the commissioning mother's entitlement to maternity leave cannot be denied only on the ground that she did not bear the child. This is dehors the fact that a commissioning mother may require to be at the bed side of the **surrogate** mother, in a given situation, even at the pre-natal stage.

Undoubtedly, the fact that the **surrogate** mother carried the pregnancy to full term, involved physiological changes to her body, which were not experienced by the commissioning mother but, from this, could one possibly conclude that her emotional involvement was any less if, not more, than the **surrogate** mother?

Central Civil Services (Leave) Rules, 1972:

The word 'maternity' has not been defined in the Central Civil Services (Leave) Rules, 1972 (in short the Leave Rules. Rule 43, which makes provision for maternity, for the sake of convenience, is extracted hereinbelow:

"...43. Maternity Leave:

(1) A female Government servant (including an apprentice) with less than two surviving children may be granted maternity leave by an authority competent to grant leave for a period of (180 days) from the date of its commencement.

(2) During such period, she shall be paid leave salary equal to the pay drawn immediately before proceeding on leave. NOTE :- In the case of a person to whom Employees' State Insurance Act, 1948 (34 of 1948), applies, the amount of leave salary payable under this rule shall be reduced by the amount of benefit payable under the said Act

for the corresponding period.

(3) Maternity leave not exceeding 45 days may also be granted to a female Government servant (irrespective of the number of surviving children) during the entire service of that female Government in case of miscarriage including abortion on production of medical certificate as laid down in Rule 19: `Provided that the maternity leave granted and availed of before the commencement of the CCS(Leave) Amendment Rules, 1995, shall not be taken into account for the purpose of this sub-rule'.

(4) (a) Maternity leave may be combined with leave of any other kind. (b) Notwithstanding the requirement of production of medical certificate contained in sub-rule (1) of Rule 30 or sub-rule (1) of Rule 31, leave of the kind due and admissible (including commuted leave for a period not exceeding 60 days and leave not due) up to a maximum of one year may, if applied for, be granted in continuation of maternity leave granted under sub-rule (1).

(5) Maternity leave shall not be debited against the leave account..."

A perusal of Rule 43 would show that a female employee including an apprentice with less than two surviving children, can avail of maternity leave for 180 days from the date of its commencement. Sub-rule (3) of Rule 43 is indicative of the fact that where the female employee has suffered a miscarriage, including abortion, she can avail of maternity leave not exceeding 45 days. Importantly, clause (a) of sub-rule (4) of Rule 43, states that maternity leave can be combined with leave of any other kind. Furthermore, under clause (b) of sub-rule (4) such a female employee is entitled to leave of the kind referred to in Rule 31(1) notwithstanding the requirement to produce a medical certificate, subject to a maximum of two years, if applied for, in continuation of maternity leave granted to her. Sub-rule (5) of Rule 43 states that, maternity leave shall not be debited against leave account.

There are three other Rules. Rules 43-A, 43-AA and 43-B.

Rule 43-A[70] deals with paternity leave available to a male employee

---

70 43-A. Paternity leave:

for the defined period, where "his wife" is confined on account of child birth. The said Rule allows a male employee, including an apprentice, with less than two surviving children, to avail of 15 days leave during the confinement of his wife for child birth, that is, up to 15 days "before" or "up to 6 months" from the date of delivery of the child.

Sub-rule (4) of Rule 43-A makes it clear that if paternity leave is not availed of within the period specified above, such leave shall be treated as lapsed.

Like in the case of a female employee, paternity leave can be combined with leave of any other kind, and the said leave is not debited against the male employee's leave account. This position emanates upon reading of sub-rule (3) and sub-rule (4) of Rule 43-A above.

Rule 43-AA[471] deals with paternity leave made available, to a male

---

(1) A male Government servant (including an apprentice) with less than two surviving children, may be granted Paternity Leave by an authority competent to grant leave for a period of 15 days, during the confinement of his wife for childbirth, i.e., up to 15 days before, or up to six months from the date of delivery of the child.
(2) During such period of 15 days, he shall be paid leave salary equal to the pay drawn immediately before proceeding on leave.
(3) The paternity Leave may be combined with leave of any other kind.
(4) The paternity leave shall not be debited against the leave account.
(5) If Paternity Leave is not availed of within the period specified in sub-rule (1), such leave shall be treated as lapsed.
NOTE:- The Paternity Leave shall not normally be refused under any circumstances.]

71 43-AA. Paternity Leave for Child Adoption. -
(1) A male Government servant (including an apprentice) with less than two surviving children, on valid adoption of a child below the age of one year, may be granted Paternity Leave for a period of 15 days within a period of six months from the date of valid adoption.
(2) During such period of 15 days, he shall be paid leave salary equal to the pay drawn immediately before proceeding on leave.
(3) The paternity leave may be combined with leave of any other kind.
(4) The Paternity Leave shall not be debited against the leave account.
(5) If Paternity leave is not availed of within the period specified in sub-rule (1) such leave shall be treated as lapsed.
[Note 1]: - The Paternity Leave shall not normally be refused under any

employee, for the defined period, albeit from the date of "valid adoption".

The aforementioned rule is parimateria[72] with Rule 43-A, in all other aspects; the only difference being that the paternity leave of 15 days available to the male employee should be availed of within 6 months from the date of a valid adoption.

Under the Leave Rules, a female employee is also entitled to leave if she were to adopt a child as against taking recourse to the surrogacy route. In other words, there is a provision in the Leave Rules for Child Adoption Leave. The relevant provision in this behalf is made in Rule 43-B[73].

---

circumstances.]

[Note 2]: - "Child" for the purpose of this rule will include a child taken as ward by the Government servant, under the Guardians and Wards Act, 1890 or the personal law applicable to that Government servant, provided such a ward lives with the Government servant and is treated as a member of the family and provided such Government servant has, through a special will, conferred upon that ward the same status as that of a natural born child.]

72 **Meaning of PariMateria:**
A designation applied to statutes or general laws that were enacted at different time but pertain to the same subject or object.
Statutes in pari materia must be interpreted in light of each other since they have a common purpose for comparable events or items.

73 43-B. Leave to a female Government servant on adoption of a child:
(1) A female Government servant, with fewer than two surviving children, on valid adoption of a child below the age of one year may be granted child adoption leave, by an authority competent to grant leave, for a period of [180 days] immediately after the date of valid adoption.
(2) During the period of child adoption leave, she shall be paid leave salary equal to the pay drawn immediately before proceeding on leave.
(3) (a) Child adoption leave may be combined with leave of any other kind.
(b) In continuation of the child adoption leave granted under sub-rule (1), a female Government servant on valid adoption of a child may also be granted, if applied for, leave of the kind due and admissible (including leave not due and commuted leave not exceeding 60 days without production of medical certificate) for a period upto one year reduced by the age of the adopted child on the date of valid adoption, without taking into account child adoption leave. Provided that this facility shall not be admissible in case she is already having two surviving children at the time of adoption.
(4) Child adoption leave shall not be debited against the leave account.]

Rule 43-B, which enables the female employee with fewer than two surviving children, to avail of child adoption leave for a period of 180 days affixes, inter alia, a condition that there should be in place a "valid adoption" of a child below the age of one year. The period of 180 days commences immediately after the date of valid adoption. [See sub-rule (1) of Rule 43-B]

Clause (a) of sub-rule (3) of Rule 43-B enables a female employee to combine child adoption leave with leave of any other kind. Clause (b) of sub-rule (3) of Rule 43-B, entitles a female employee in continuation of child adoption leave granted under sub-rule (1), on valid adoption of a child to apply for leave of the kind due and admissible (including leave not due and commuted leave not exceeding 60 days without production of medical certificates) for a period up to one year, albeit reduced by the age of adopted child on the date of "valid adoption". In other words, this sub-rule allows a female employee to apply for any other leave which is due and admissible in addition to child adoption leave. There is, however, a proviso added to the said sub-rule which prevents a female employee to avail of such leave if she already has two surviving children at the time of adoption.

As in the other rules, child adoption leave is not to be debited against the leave account.

Thus, a reading of Rule 43 would show that while it is indicated in sub-rule (1) as to when the period of leave is to commence, that is,

---

[Note: - "Child" for the purpose of this rule will include a child taken as ward by the Government servant, under the Guardians and Wards Act, 1890 or the personal Law applicable to that Government servant, provided such a ward lives with the Government servant and is treated as a member of the family and provided such Government servant has, through a special will, conferred upon that ward the same status as that of a natural born child.] The said Rule was substituted by notification dated 31.03.2006 and was published in the gazette of India on 27.04.2006; to take effect from 31.03.2006. It appears that prior to the insertion of Rule 43-B, the said rule was numbered as 43-A and was inserted vide notification dated 22.10.1990, which was published in the gazette of India, on 26.01.1991. The said notification was, however, substituted by another notification dated 04.03.1992, which in turn was published in the gazette of India on 14.03.1992.

from the date of maternity; the expression 'maternity' by itself has not been defined. As a matter of fact, sub-rule (3) of Rule 43 shows that if the pregnancy is not carried to full term on account of miscarriage, which may include abortion, a female employee is entitled to leave not exceeding 45 days.

There are two ways of looking at Rule 43. One, that the word, 'maternity' should be given the same meaning, which one may argue inheres in it, on a reading of sub-rule (3) of Rule 43; which is the notion of child bearing. The other, that the word "maternity", as appearing in sub-rule (1) of Rule 43, with advancement of science and technology, should be given a meaning, which includes within it, the concept of motherhood attained via the surrogacy route. The latter appears to be more logical if, the language of Rule 43-A, which deals with paternity leave, is contrasted with sub-rule (1) of Rule 43. Rule 43-A makes it clear that a male employee would get 15 days of leave "during the confinement of his wife for child birth", either 15 days prior to the event, or thereafter, i.e. after child birth, subject to the said leave being availed of within 6 months of the delivery of the child.

There is no express stipulation in sub-rule (1) of Rule 43 to the effect that the female employee (applying for leave) should also be one who is carrying the child. The said aspect while being implicit in sub-rule (1) of Rule 43, does not exclude attainment of motherhood via surrogacy. The attributes such as "confinement" of the female employee during child birth or the conditionality of division of leave into periods before and after child birth do not find mention in Rule 43(1).

Decision by High Court:

In court opinion, where a surrogacy arrangement is in place, the commissioning mother continues to remain the legal mother of the child, both during and after the pregnancy. To cite an example : suppose on account of a disagreement between the **surrogate** mother and the commissioning parents, the **surrogate** mother takes a unilateral decision to terminate the pregnancy, albeit within the period permissible in law for termination of pregnancy, the commissioning parents would have a legal right to restrain the **surrogate** mother from taking any such action which may be detrimental to the interest of the child. The legal basis for the court to entertain such a plea would, in court view, be, amongst others, the fact that the commissioning mother is the legal mother of the child. The basis for reaching such a conclusion is that, surrogacy, is recognized as a lawful agreement in the eyes of law in this country[74]. In some jurisdictions though, a formal parental order is required after child birth.

Therefore, according to court, maternity is established vis-a-vis the commissioning mother, once the child is conceived, albeit in a womb, other than that of the commissioning mother.

It is to be appreciated that Maternity, in law and/or on facts can be established in any one of the three situations: First, where a female employee herself conceives and carries the child. Second, where a female employee engages the services of another female to conceive a child with or without the genetic material being supplied by her and/or her male partner. Third, where female employee adopts a child.

In so far as the third circumstance is concerned, a specific rule is available for availing leave, is provided for in Rule 43-B. In so far as the first situation is concerned, it is covered under sub-rule (1) of Rule 43. However, as regards the second situation, it would necessarily have to be read into sub-rule (1) of Rule 43.

To confine sub-rule (1) of Rule 43 to only to that situation, where the female employee herself carries a child, would be turning a blind eye to the advancement that science has made in the meanwhile. On the other hand, if a truncated meaning is given to the word 'maternity', it would result in depriving a large number of women of their right to avail of a vital service benefit, only on account of the choice that they would have exercised in respect of child birth.

In a surrogacy arrangement, the concern of the commissioning parents, in particular, the commissioning mother is to a large extent, focused on the child carried by the gestational mother. There may

---

74 [See Baby Manji Yamada v. Union of India, (2008) 13 SCC 518]

be myriad situations in which the interest of the child, while still in the womb of the gestational mother, may require to be safeguarded by the commissioning mother. To cite an example, a situation may arise where a commissioning mother may need to attend to the **surrogate**/gestational mother[75] during the term of pregnancy; because the latter may be bereft[76] of the necessary wherewithal. The lack of wherewithal could be of : financial nature (the arrangement in place may not suffice for whatever reasons), physical condition or emotional support or even a combination of one or more factors stated above. In such like circumstances, the commissioning mother can function effectively, as a care-giver, only if, she is in a position to exercise the right to take maternity leave. To my mind, to curtail the commissioning mother's entitlement to leave, on the ground that she has not conceived the child, would work, both to her detriment, as well as, that of the child.

The likelihood of such right, if accorded to the commissioning mother, being misused can always be curtailed by the competent leave sanctioning authority.

At the time of sanctioning leave the competent authority can always seek information with regard to circumstances which obtain in a given case, where application for grant of maternity leave is made. The competent authority's scrutiny, to my mind, would be keener and perhaps more detailed, where leave is sought by the commissioning mother at the pre-natal stage, as against post-natal stage. If conditions do not commend that leave be given at the pre-natal stage, then the same can be declined.

In so far as post-natal stage is concerned, ordinarily, leave cannot be declined as, under most surrogacy arrangements, once the child is born, its custody is immediately handed over to the commissioning parents. The commissioning mother, post the birth of the child,

---

75 Meaning of gestational other: who carries a fertilized embryo to completion of pregnancy

76 **Meaning of bereft:**
   a. Deprived of something
   b. Lacking something needed or expected

would, in all probability, have to play a very crucial role in rearing the child.

Best interests of child [is] paramount

In all matters concerning the care, protection and well-being of a child the standard that the child's best interest is of paramount importance must be applied.

Surrogacy agreements are regulated by the Children's Act.

The surrogacy agreement specifically provides that the newly born child is immediately handed to the commissioning parents. During his evidence the applicant explained that for various reasons that he and his spouse had decided that he, the applicant, would perform the role usually performed by the birthmother by taking immediate responsibility for the child and accordingly he would apply for maternity leave. The applicant explained that the child was taken straight from the **surrogate** and given to him and that the **surrogate** did not even have sight of the child. Only one commissioning parent was permitted to be present at the birth and he had accepted this role.

Given these circumstances there is no reason why an employee in the position of the applicant should not be entitled to "maternity leave" and equally no reason why such maternity leave should not be for the same duration as the maternity leave to which a natural mother is entitled"

In our Constitution, under Article 39 (f)[77], which falls in part IV,

---

77 **Article 39 in The Constitution of India 1949**
39. Certain principles of policy to be followed by the State: The State shall, in particular, direct its policy towards securing
(a) that the citizens, men and women equally, have the right to an adequate means to livelihood;
(b) that the ownership and control of the material resources of the community are so distributed as best to subserve the common good;
(c) that the operation of the economic system does not result in the concentration of wealth and means of production to the common detriment;
(d) that there is equal pay for equal work for both men and women;
(e) that the health and strength of workers, men and women, and the tender

under the heading Directive Principles of the States policy, the state is obliged to, inter alia, ensure that the children are given opportunities and facilities to develop in a healthy manner. Similarly, under Article 45[78], State has an obligation to provide early childhood care.

Non-provision of leave to a commissioning mother, who is a employee, would be in derogation of the stated Directive Principles of State Policy[79] as contained in the Constitution.

Court reached to the following conclusion:

(i). A female employee, who is the commissioning mother, would be entitled to apply for maternity leave under sub-rule (1) of Rule 43.

(ii). The competent authority based on material placed before it would decide on the timing and the period for which maternity leave ought to be granted to a commissioning mother who adopts the surrogacy route.

(iii) The scrutiny would be keener and detailed, when leave is sought by a female employee, who is the commissioning mother, at the pre-

---

age of children are not abused and that citizens are not forced by economic necessity to enter avocations unsuited to their age or strength;

(f) that children are given opportunities and facilities to develop in a healthy manner and in conditions of freedom and dignity and that childhood and youth are protected against exploitation and against moral and material abandonment

78 **Article 45 in The Constitution of India 1949**
45. Provision for free and compulsory education for children The State shall endeavour to provide, within a period of ten years from the commencement of this Constitution, for free and compulsory education for all children until they complete the age of fourteen years

79 The **Directive Principles of State Policy** are guidelines/principles given to the central and state governments of India, to be kept in mind while framing laws and policies. These provisions, contained in Part IV of the Constitution of India, are not enforceable by any court, but the principles laid down therein are considered fundamental in the governance of the country, making it the duty of the State to apply these principles in making laws to establish a just society in the country. The principles have been inspired by the Directive Principles given in the Constitution of Ireland and also by the principles of Gandhism; and relate to social justice, economic welfare, foreign policy, and legal and administrative matters.

natal stage. In case maternity leave is declined at the pre-natal stage, the competent authority would pass a reasoned order having regard to the material, if any, placed before it, by the female employee, who seeks to avail maternity leave. In a situation where both the commissioning mother and the **surrogate** mother are employees, who are otherwise eligible for leave (one on the ground that she is a commissioning mother and the other on the ground that she is the pregnant women), a suitable adjustment would be made by the competent authority.

(iv). In so far as grant of leave qua post-natal period is concerned, the competent authority would ordinarily grant such leave except where there are substantial reasons for declining a request made in that behalf.

Case-5

Woman Can Seek 'Stridhan[80]' back Even if Marriage Not Dissolved[81]

Facts in Nutshell:

The Appellant[82]-- **Krishna Bhatacharjee** having lost the battle for getting her Stridhan back from her husband, the first Respondent[83]---Sarathi Choudhury and Ors., before the learned Magistrate on the ground that the claim preferred Under Section 12[84] of the Protection

---

80 Stridhan is a traditional practice that was primarily meant to provide women with some level of economic security in adverse situations like divorce, widowhood, etc.

81 Appellants: **Krishna Bhatacharjee Vs.**Respondent: **Sarathi Choudhury and Ors.**
Hon'ble Judges/Coram: Dipak Misra and Prafulla C. Pant, JJ., Supreme Court of India Decided On: 20.11.2015, MANU/SC/1330/2015

82 **Meaning of Appellant:**
One who appeals a court decision.

83 **Meaning of Respondent:**
The defending party in certain legal proceedings, as in a case brought by petition.

84 **Section 12 in The Protection of Women from Domestic Violence Act, 2005**

of Women from Domestic Violence Act, 2005 (for short, 'the 2005 Act') was not entertainable as she had ceased[85] to be an "aggrieved person" Under Section 2(a)[86] of the 2005 Act and further that the claim as put forth was barred by limitation; preferred an appeal[87] before the learned Additional Sessions Judge who concurred with the view

---

12. Application to Magistrate.—

(1) An aggrieved person or a Protection Officer or any other person on behalf of the aggrieved person may present an application to the Magistrate seeking one or more reliefs under this Act: Provided that before passing any order on such application, the Magistrate shall take into consideration any domestic incident report received by him from the Protection Officer or the service provider.

(2) The relief sought for under sub-section (1) may include a relief for issuance of an order for payment of compensation or damages without prejudice to the right of such person to institute a suit for compensation or damages for the injuries caused by the acts of domestic violence committed by the respondent: Provided that where a decree for any amount as compensation or damages has been passed by any court in favour of the aggrieved person, the amount, if any, paid or payable in pursuance of the order made by the Magistrate under this Act shall be set off against the amount payable under such decree and the decree shall, notwithstanding anything contained in the Code of Civil Procedure, 1908 (5 of 1908), or any other law for the time being in force, be executable for the balance amount, if any, left after s uch set off.

(3) Every application under sub-section (1) shall be in such form and contain such particulars as may be prescribed or as nearly as possible thereto.

(4) The Magistrate shall fix the first date of hearing, which shall not ordinarily be beyond three days from the date of receipt of the application by the court.

(5) The Magistrate shall endeavour to dispose of every application made under sub-section (1) within a period of sixty days from the date of its first hearing.

85 **Meaning of cease:**

1. To come to an end; stop

2. To stop performing an activity or action; desist

86 Section 2 in The Protection of Women from Domestic Violence Act, 2005

2. Definitions.—In this Act, unless the context otherwise requires,—

(a) "aggrieved person" means any woman who is, or has been, in a domestic relationship with the respondent and who alleges to have been subjected to any act of domestic violence by the respondent

87 **Meaning of appeal:**

a. A higher court's review of the correctness of a decision by a lower court.

b. A case so reviewed.

expressed by the learned Magistrate, and being determined to get her lawful claim, she, despite the repeated non-success, approached the High Court of Tripura, Agartala in Criminal Revision with the hope that she will be victorious in the war to get her own property, but the High Court without much analysis declined to interfere by passing an order with Spartan[88] austerity[89] possibly thinking lack of reasoning is equivalent to a magnificent virtue and that had led the agonised and perturbed wife/Appellant to prefer the appeal by way of special leave petition[90] before the supreme court.

Brief Facts:

The marriage between the Appellant--Wife and the Respondent No. 1---husband was solemnised on 27.11.2005 and they lived as husband and wife. As the allegations proceed, there was demand of dowry by the husband including his relatives and, demands not being satisfied, the Appellant was driven out from the matrimonial home. However, due to intervention of the elderly people of the locality, there was some kind of conciliation[91] as a consequence of which both the husband and the wife stayed in a rented house for two months. With

---

88 **Meaning of Spartan:**
   a. Rigorously self-disciplined or self-restrained.

   b. Simple, frugal, or austere

89 **Meaning of austerity:**
   1. the state or quality of being austere

   2. an austere habit, practice, or act

90 **Article 136 in The Constitution Of India 1949**
   136. Special leave to appeal by the Supreme Court
   (1) Notwithstanding anything in this Chapter, the Supreme Court may, in its discretion, grant special leave to appeal from any judgment, decree, determination, sentence or order in any cause or matter passed or made by any court or tribunal in the territory of India
   (2) Nothing in clause (1) shall apply to any judgment, determination, sentence or order passed or made by any court or tribunal constituted by or under any law relating to the Armed Forces

91 **Meaning of conciliate:**
   1. To overcome the distrust or animosity of; appease.

   2. To regain or try to regain (friendship or goodwill) by pleasant behavior.

the efflux[92] of time, the husband filed a petition[93] seeking judicial separation[94] before the Family Court and eventually the said prayer was granted by the learned Judge, Family Court. After the judicial separation, on 22.5.2010 the Appellant--wife filed an application Under Section 12 of the 2005 Act before the Child Development Protection Officer (CDPO), , Agartala, Tripura seeking necessary help as per the provisions contained in the 2005 Act. She sought seizure of Stridhan articles from the possession of the husband. The application which was made before the CDPO was forwarded by the said authority to the learned Chief Judicial Magistrate, Agartala Sadar, West Tripura by letter dated 1.6.2010. The learned Magistrate issued notice to the Respondent who filed his written objections on 14.2.2011.

Before the learned Magistrate it was contended by the Respondent--husband that the application preferred by the wife was barred by limitation and that she could not have raised claim as regards Stridhan after the decree[95] of judicial separation passed by the competent court.

Decision by learned Magistrate, Additional Sessions Judge& High Court:

The learned Magistrate taking into consideration the admitted

---

92 **Meaning of efflux:**
   1. A flowing outward.
   2. Something that flows out or forth; an effluence.

93 **Meaning of petition:**
   a. A formal written application seeking a court's intervention and action on a matter.
   b. A pleading initiating a legal case in some civil courts

94 **Legal separation** (sometimes "judicial separation", "separate maintenance", "divorce *a mensa et thoro*", or "divorce from bed-and-board") is a legal process by which a married couple may formalize a *de facto* separation while remaining legally married. A legal separation is granted in the form of a court order.

95 **Meaning of decree:**
   a. The judgment of a court of equity.
   b. The judgment of a court.

fact that Respondent and the Appellant had entered into wedlock treated her as an "aggrieved person", but opined that no "domestic relationship" as defined Under Section 2(f)[96] of the 2005 Act existed between the parties and, therefore, wife was not entitled to file the application Under Section 12 of the 2005 Act. The learned Magistrate came to hold that though the parties had not been divorced but the decree of judicial separation would be an impediment for entertaining the application and being of this view, he opined that no domestic relationship subsisted under the 2005 Act and hence, no relief could be granted.

The aggrieved wife preferred criminal appeal which was decided by the learned Additional Sessions Judge, Agartala holding, inter alia[97], that the object of the 2005 Act is primarily to give immediate relief to the victims; that as per the decision of Supreme Court in *Inderjit Singh Grewal v. State of Punjab*[98] that Section 468[99] of the Code of Criminal Procedure applies to the proceedings under the 2005 Act and, therefore, her application was barred by time. Being of this view,

---

96 (f) "domestic relationship" means a relationship between two persons who live or have, at any point of time, lived together in a shared household, when they are related by consanguinity, marriage, or through a relationship in the nature of marriage, adoption or are family members living together as a joint family

97 **Meaning of inter-alia:**
Among other things.

98 (2011) 12 SCC 588

99 Section 468 in The Code Of Criminal Procedure, 1973
468. Bar to taking cognizance after lapse of the period of limitation.
(1) Except as otherwise provided elsewhere in this Code, no Court shall take cognizance of an offence of the category specified in sub- section (2), after the expiry of the period of limitation.
(2) The period of limitation shall be-
(a) six months, if the offence is punishable with fine only
(b) one year, if the offence is punishable with imprisonment for a term not exceeding one year;
(c) three years, if the offence is punishable with imprisonment for term exceeding one year but not exceeding three years.
(3) 1 For the purposes of this section, the period of limitation in relation to offences which may be tried together, shall be determined with reference to the offence which is punishable with the more severe punishment or, as the case may be, the most severe punishment.]

the appellate court dismissed the appeal.

On a revision petition High Court, after referring to the decision in *Inderjit Singh Grewal v. State of Punjab*[100]stated that the wife had filed a criminal case Under Section 498(A)[101] Indian Penal Code in the year 2006 and the husband had obtained a decree of judicial separation in 2008, and hence, the proceedings under the 2005 Act was barred by limitation. That apart, it has also in a way expressed the view that the proceedings under the 2005 Act was not maintainable.

Domestic Violence Act, 2005:

Section 2(a) defines "aggrieved person" which means any woman who is, or has been, in a domestic relationship with the Respondent and who alleges to have been subjected to any act of domestic violence by the Respondent.

Section 2(f) defines "domestic relationship" which means a relationship between two persons who live or have, at any point of time, lived together in a shared household, when they are related by consanguinity, marriage, or through a relationship in the nature of marriage, adoption or are family members living together as a joint family. Section 2(g) defines the term "domestic violence" which has been assigned and given the same meaning as in Section 3. Sub-section (iv) of Section 3 deals with "economic abuse".

---

100 (2011) 12 SCC 588

101 Section 498A in The Indian Penal Code

498A. Husband or relative of husband of a woman subjecting her to cruelty.—Whoever, being the husband or the relative of the husband of a woman, subjects such woman to cruelty shall be punished with imprisonment for a term which may extend to three years and shall also be liable to fine. Explanation.—For the purpose of this section, "cruelty" means—

(a) any wilful conduct which is of such a nature as is likely to drive the woman to commit suicide or to cause grave injury or danger to life, limb or health (whether mental or physical) of the woman; or

(b) harassment of the woman where such harassment is with a view to coercing her or any person related to her to meet any unlawful demand for any property or valuable security or is on account of failure by her or any person related to her to meet such demand.

Economic Abuse under Domestic Violence Act, 2005:

Section 3. Definition of domestic violence.

(iv) "economic abuse" includes-

(a) deprivation of all or any economic or financial resources to which the aggrieved person is entitled under any law or custom whether payable under an order of a court or otherwise or which the aggrieved person requires out of necessity including, but not limited to, household necessities for the aggrieved person and her children, if any, stridhan, property, jointly or separately owned by the aggrieved person, payment of rental related to the shared household and maintenance;

(b) disposal of household effects, any alienation of assets whether movable or immovable, valuables, shares, securities, bonds and the like or other property in which the aggrieved person has an interest or is entitled to use by virtue of the domestic relationship or which may be reasonably required by the aggrieved person or her children or her stridhan or any other property jointly or separately held by the aggrieved person; and

(c) prohibition or restriction to continued access to resources or facilities which the aggrieved person is entitled to use or enjoy by virtue of the domestic relationship including access to the shared household.

Explanation II.-For the purpose of determining whether any act, omission, commission or conduct of the Respondent constitutes "domestic violence" under this section, the overall facts and circumstances of the case shall be taken into consideration.

Section 8(1)[102] empowers the State Government to appoint such

102 Section 8 in The Protection of Women from Domestic Violence Act, 2005
   8. Appointment of Protection Officers.—
   (1) The State Government shall, by notification, appoint such number of Protection Officers in each district as it may consider necessary and shall also notify the area or areas within which a Protection Officer shall exercise the powers and perform the duties conferred on him by or under this Act.
   (2) The Protection Officers shall as far as possible be women and shall possess

number of Protection Officers in each district as it may consider necessary and also to notify the area or areas within which a Protection Officer shall exercise the powers and perform the duties conferred on him by or under the 2005 Act. The provision, as is manifest, is mandatory and the State Government is under the legal obligation to appoint such Protection Officers.

Section 12 deals with application to Magistrate. Sub-sections (1) and (2) being relevant are reproduced below:

Section 12. Application to Magistrate.-(1) An aggrieved person or a Protection Officer or any other person on behalf of the aggrieved person may present an application to the Magistrate seeking one or more reliefs under this Act: Provided that before passing any order on such application, the Magistrate shall take into consideration any domestic incident report received by him from the Protection Officer or the service provider.

(2) The relief sought for Under Sub-section (1) may include a relief for issuance of an order for payment of compensation or damages without prejudice to the right of such person to institute a suit for compensation or damages for the injuries caused by the acts of domestic violence committed by the Respondent: Provided that where a decree for any amount as compensation or damages has been passed by any court in favour of the aggrieved person, the amount, if any, paid or payable in pursuance of the order made by the Magistrate under this Act shall be set off against the amount payable under such decree and the decree shall, notwithstanding anything contained in the Code of Civil Procedure, 1908 (5 of 1908), or any other law for the time being in force, be executable for the balance amount, if any, left after such set off.

Section 18[103] deals with passing of protection orders by the Magistrate.

---

such qualifications and experience as may be prescribed.

(3) The terms and conditions of service of the Protection Officer and the other officers subordinate to him shall be such as may be prescribed.

103 Section 18 in The Protection of Women from Domestic Violence Act, 2005

18. Protection orders.—The Magistrate may, after giving the aggrieved person and the respondent an opportunity of being heard and on being prima facie

Section19[104] deals with the residence orders Section 20[105] deals with monetary reliefs. Section 28[106] deals with procedure and stipulates that all proceedings Under Sections 12,18, 19, 20, 21[107], 22[108] and 23[109]

---

satisfied that domestic violence has taken place or is likely to take place, pass a protection order in favour of the aggrieved person.

104 Section 19 in The Protection of Women from Domestic Violence Act, 2005
    Section 19: Resident Orders...

105 Section 20 in The Protection of Women from Domestic Violence Act, 2005
    20. Monetary reliefs.—

106 Section 28 in The Protection of Women from Domestic Violence Act, 2005
    28. Procedure.—
    (1) Save as otherwise provided in this Act, all proceedings under sections 12, 18, 19, 20, 21, 22 and 23 and offences under section 31 shall be governed by the provisions of the Code of Criminal Procedure, 1973 (2 of 1974).
    (2) Nothing in sub-section (1) shall prevent the court from laying down its own procedure for disposal of an application under section 12 or under sub-section (2) of section 23.

107 Section 21 in The Protection of Women from Domestic Violence Act, 2005
    21. Custody orders.—Notwithstanding anything contained in any other law for the time being in force, the Magistrate may, at any stage of hearing of the application for protection order or for any other relief under this Act grant temporary custody of any child or children to the aggrieved person or the person making an application on her behalf and specify, if necessary, the arrangements for visit of such child or children by the respondent: Provided that if the Magistrate is of the opinion that any visit of the respondent may be harmful to the interests of the child or children, the Magistrate shall refuse to allow such visit.

108 Section 22 in The Protection of Women from Domestic Violence Act, 2005
    22. Compensation orders.—In addition to other reliefs as may be granted under this Act, the Magistrate may on an application being made by the aggrieved person, pass an order directing the respondent to pay compensation and damages for the injuries, including mental torture and emotional distress, caused by the acts of domestic violence committed by that respondent.

109 Section 23 in The Protection of Women from Domestic Violence Act, 2005
    23. Power to grant interim and ex parte orders.—
    (1) In any proceeding before him under this Act, the Magistrate may pass such interim order as he deems just and proper.
    (2) If the Magistrate is satisfied that an application prima facie discloses that the respondent is committing, or has committed an act of domestic violence or that there is a likelihood that the respondent may commit an act of domestic violence, he may grant an ex parte order on the basis of the affidavit in

and offences Under Section 31[110] shall be governed by the provisions of the Code of Criminal Procedure, 1973. Section 36[111]lays down that the provisions of the 2005 Act shall be in addition to, and not in derogation of the provisions of any other law, for the time being in force.

Case Laws referred:

In *V.D. Bhanot v. Savita Bhanot*[112] the question arose whether the provisions of the 2005 Act can be made applicable in relation to an incident that had occurred prior to the coming into force of the said Act. The High Court rejected the stand of the Respondent--wife therein that the provisions of the 2005 Act cannot be invoked if the occurrence had taken place prior to the coming into force of the 2005 Act. Supreme Court while dealing with the same held that it was with the view of protecting the rights of women Under Articles

---

such form, as may be prescribed, of the aggrieved person under section 18, section 19, section 20, section 21 or, as the case may be, section 22 against the respondent.

110 Section 31 in The Protection of Women from Domestic Violence Act, 2005
31. Penalty for breach of protection order by respondent.—
(1) A breach of protection order, or of an interim protection order, by the respondent shall be an offence under this Act and shall be punishable with imprisonment of either description for a term which may extend to one year, or with fine which may extend to twenty thousand rupees, or with both.
(2) The offence under sub-section (1) shall as far as practicable be tried by the Magistrate who had passed the order, the breach of which has been alleged to have been caused by the accused.
(3) While framing charges under sub-section (1), the Magistrates may also frame charges under section 498A of the Indian Penal Code (45 of 1860) or any other provision of that Code or the Dowry Prohibition Act, 1961 (28 of 1961), as the case may be, if the facts disclose the commission of an offence under those provisions.

111 Section 36 in The Protection of Women from Domestic Violence Act, 2005
36. Act not in derogation of any other law.—The provisions of this Act shall be in addition to, and not in derogation of the provisions of any other law, for the time being in force.

112 (2012) 3 SCC 183

14[113], 15[114] and 21[115] of the Constitution that Parliament enacted the 2005 Act in order to provide for some effective protection of rights guaranteed under the Constitution to women, who are victims of any kind of violence occurring within the family and matters connected therewith and incidental thereto, and to provide an efficient and expeditious[116] civil remedy to them and further that a petition under the provisions of the 2005 Act is maintainable even if the acts of domestic violence had been committed prior to the coming into force of the said Act, notwithstanding the fact that in the past she had lived together with her husband in a shared household, but was no more living with him, at the time when the Act came into force.

---

113 Article 14 in The Constitution Of India 1949

14. Equality before law The State shall not deny to any person equality before the law or the equal protection of the laws within the territory of India Prohibition of discrimination on grounds of religion, race, caste, sex or place of birth

114 Article 15 in The Constitution Of India 1949

15. Prohibition of discrimination on grounds of religion, race, caste, sex or place of birth

(1) The State shall not discriminate against any citizen on grounds only of religion, race, caste, sex, place of birth or any of them

(2) No citizen shall, on grounds only of religion, race, caste, sex, place of birth or any of them, be subject to any disability, liability, restriction or condition with regard to

(a) access to shops, public restaurants, hotels and palaces of public entertainment; or

(b) the use of wells, tanks, bathing ghats, roads and places of public resort maintained wholly or partly out of State funds or dedicated to the use of the general public

(3) Nothing in this article shall prevent the State from making any special provision for women and children

(4) Nothing in this article or in clause (2) of Article 29 shall prevent the State from making any special provision for the advancement of any socially and educationally backward classes of citizens or for the Scheduled Castes and the Scheduled Tribes

115 Article 21 in The Constitution Of India 1949

21. Protection of life and personal liberty No person shall be deprived of his life or personal liberty except according to procedure established by law

116 Meaning of expeditious:

Acting or done with speed and efficiency

In *Saraswathy v. Babu*[117] a two-Judge Bench of Supreme held thus:

Supreme Court was of the view that the act of the Respondent-- husband squarely comes within the ambit of Section 3[118] of the DVA,

---

117 (2014) 3 SCC 712

118 Section 3 in The Protection of Women from Domestic Violence Act, 2005
3. Definition of domestic violence.—For the purposes of this Act, any act, omission or commission or conduct of the respondent shall constitute domestic violence in case it—
(a) harms or injures or endangers the health, safety, life, limb or well-being, whether mental or physical, of the aggrieved person or tends to do so and includes causing physical abuse, sexual abuse, verbal and emotional abuse and economic abuse; or
(b) harasses, harms, injures or endangers the aggrieved person with a view to coerce her or any other person related to her to meet any unlawful demand for any dowry or other property or valuable security; or
(c) has the effect of threatening the aggrieved person or any person related to her by any conduct mentioned in clause (a) or clause (b); or
(d) otherwise injures or causes harm, whether physical or mental, to the aggrieved person. Explanation I.—For the purposes of this section,—
(i) "physical abuse" means any act or conduct which is of such a nature as to cause bodily pain, harm, or danger to life, limb, or health or impair the health or development of the aggrieved person and includes assault, criminal intimidation and criminal force;
(ii) "sexual abuse" includes any conduct of a sexual nature that abuses, humiliates, degrades or otherwise violates the dignity of woman;
(iii) "verbal and emotional abuse" includes—
(a) insults, ridicule, humiliation, name calling and insults or ridicule specially with regard to not having a child or a male child; and
(b) repeated threats to cause physical pain to any person in whom the aggrieved person is interested.
(iv) "economic abuse" includes—
(a) deprivation of all or any economic or financial resources to which the aggrieved person is entitled under any law or custom whether payable under an order of a court or otherwise or which the aggrieved person requires out of necessity including, but not limited to, household necessities for the aggrieved person and her children, if any, stridhan, property, jointly or separately owned by the aggrieved person, payment of rental related to the shared household and maintenance;
(b) disposal of household effects, any alienation of assets whether movable or immovable, valuables, shares, securities, bonds and the like or other property in which the aggrieved person has an interest or is entitled to use by virtue of the domestic relationship or which may be reasonably required by the

2005, which defines "domestic violence" in wide terms. The High Court made an apparent error in holding that the conduct of the parties prior to the coming into force of the DVA, 2005 cannot be taken into consideration while passing an order.

Supreme Court held that Appellant wife having being harassed since 2000 was entitled for protection order and residence order Under Sections 18 and 19 of the DVA, 2005 along with the maintenance. Apart from these reliefs, she was also entitled for compensation and damages for the injuries, including mental torture and emotional distress, caused by the acts of domestic violence committed by the Respondent--- husband. Supreme Court was of the view that Appellant wife should be compensated by the respondent-- husband. Hence, the Respondent—husband was directed to pay compensation and damages to the extent of Rs. 5,00,000 in favour of the Appellant—wife by the Supreme Court.

Decision by Supreme Court:

Court was of the view that there is a distinction between a decree for divorce and decree of judicial separation; in the former, there is a severance of status and the parties do not remain as husband and wife, whereas in the later, the relationship between husband and wife continues and the legal relationship continues as it has not been snapped. Thus understood, the finding recorded by the courts (Learned magistrate, additional session judge and High court) that the parties having been judicial separated, the Appellant wife has ceased to be an "aggrieved person" was wholly unsustainable was observed by Supreme Court.

The next issue was the claim of stridhan by the wife, she was claiming to get back her stridhan. Stridhan has been described as

---

aggrieved person or her children or her stridhan or any other property jointly or separately held by the aggrieved person; and

(c) prohibition or restriction to continued access to resources or facilities which the aggrieved person is entitled to use or enjoy by virtue of the domestic relationship including access to the shared household. Explanation II.—For the purpose of determining whether any act, omission, commission or conduct of the respondent constitutes "domestic violence" under this section, the overall facts and circumstances of the case shall be taken into consideration.

saudayika by Sir Gooroodas Banerjee in "Hindu Law of Marriage and Stridhan" which is as follows:

First, take the case of property obtained by gift. Gifts of affectionate kindred[119], which are known by the name of saudayika stridhan, constitute a woman's absolute property, which she has at all times independent power to alienate, and over which her husband has only a qualified right, namely, the right of use in times of distress.

The position of stridhan of a Hindu married woman's property during coverture[120] is absolutely clear and unambiguous; she is the absolute owner of such property and can deal with it in any manner she likes--she may spend the whole of it or give it away at her own pleasure by gift or will without any reference to her husband. Ordinarily, the husband has no right or interest in it with the sole exception that in times of extreme distress, as in famine, illness or the like, the husband can utilise it but he is morally bound to restore it or its value when he is able to do so. It may be further noted that this right is purely personal to the husband and the property so received by him in marriage cannot be proceeded against even in execution of a decree for debt[121].

The properties gifted to women before the marriage, at the time of marriage or at the time of giving farewell or thereafter are her stridhana properties. It is her absolute property with all rights to dispose at her own pleasure. Husband has no control over her stridhana property. Husband may use it during the time of his distress but nonetheless he has a moral obligation to restore the same or its value to his wife. Therefore, stridhana property does not become a joint property of the wife and the husband and the husband has no title or independent dominion over the property as owner thereof.

Court further held that the wife-appellant had submitted the

---

119 **Meaning of kindred:**
  1. A group of related persons, as a clan or tribe.

  2. *(used with a pl. verb)* A person's relatives; kinfolk.

120 **Meaning of coverture:**
  The status of a married woman under common law.

121 *Pratibha Rani v. Suraj Kumar and Anr.,* (1985) 2 SCC 370

application on 22.05.2010 and the said authority had forwarded the same on 01.06.2010. In the application, the wife had mentioned that the husband had stopped payment of monthly maintenance from January 2010 and, therefore, she had been compelled to file the application for stridhan. Court was of the opinion that the application was not barred by limitation and the courts –Learned Magistrate, Additional Session Judge and High court had fallen into a grave error by dismissing the application of appellant being barred by limitation.

Consequently, the appeal was allowed and the orders passed by the High Court and the courts (Additional Session Judge and Magistrate) was set aside. The matter was remitted to the learned Magistrate to proceed with the application Under Section 12 of the 2005 DV Act, 2005 on merits.

Chapter-6

Final Judgment

IN THE HIGH COURT OF DELHI

W.P.(C) No. 10498/2015 and CM No. 44852/2016

Decided On: 05.01.2018

Appellants: Kush Kalra

Vs.

Respondent: Union of India and Ors.

Hon'ble Judges/Coram:

Gita Mittal, Actg. C.J. and C. Hari Shankar, J.

Kush Kalra vs. Union of India and Ors. (05.01.2018 - DELHC) : MANU/DE/0027/2018,

2018(167)DRJ584

2018(2)ESC842(Del)

MANU/DE/0027/2018

2018(1)SCT456(Delhi)

2018(2)SLR424

JUDGMENT

Gita Mittal, Actg. C.J.

"The subordination of one sex to the other ought to be replaced by a principle of perfect equality, admitting no power or privilege on the one side, nor disability on the other." – **John Stuart Mill**

1. This writ petition, instituted in public interest by the petitioner, complains of institutional discrimination by the respondents against women and prays for issuance of a writ in the nature of a mandamus to place female gainfully employed candidates at par with similarly placed male candidates and allowing their recruitment into the Indian Territorial Army. The writ petitioner contends that as per the advertisement put out by the respondents, there is no scope for women to join the Territorial Army as an officer, even if they are gainfully employed and within the age group of 18-42 years, while this is the eligibility condition enabling similarly placed men to join. The challenge, therefore, is premised primarily on the ground that this discrimination, based on gender, is violative of the fundamental rights guaranteed to all women under Articles 14, 15 and 16 of the Constitution of India and also impinges on their basic human rights.

2. In order to appreciate the impact of this discrimination, it is essential to understand the history of the Territorial Army, its role and structure as well as its current strength.

Historical background

3. The origin of the Territorial Army ('TA' hereafter) can be traced back to the year 1857, when it was formed and consisted of volunteers only comprising of Europeans & Anglo-Indians. On 1st October, 1920, the Indian Territorial Force Bill was passed by the British and at that time it was organized into two wings, namely, 'the Auxiliary Force' for Europeans and Anglo-Indians and 'the Indian Territorial Force' for Indian volunteers. After independence, the Territorial Army Act, 1948 came to be enacted and the TA was formally inaugurated on 9th October, 1949 by the Governor General of India Shri C. Rajagopalachari.

Role and structure of the Territorial Army

4. So far as its role is concerned, the TA is part of the regular Indian army. Its present declared role is to relieve the regular army from static duties and assist the civil administration in dealing with natural calamities and maintenance of essential services in situations when life of communities is affected or the security of the country

is threatened as well as to provide units for the regular army as and when required.

5. The respondents have also placed on record a Brochure which was issued inviting applications to the TA which informs that the TA is active in numerous fields.

6. Information regarding the structure of the TA is disclosed on its website i.e. http://territorialarmy.in/. It is disclosed that as on date, the TA has a strength of approximately 40,000 persons comprising of Departmental TA units such as units in the Railways; the Indian Oil Corporation; the Oil & Natural Gas Corporation; Telecommunications and the General Hospital. It also has Non-Departmental TA units of Infantry Bn (TA) and Ecological Bn (TA) affiliated to various infantry regiments of the Indian Army.

7. The Brochure placed on record additionally informs that the TA consists of engineer units for line of control fencing. Raising of four composite Ecological Task Force Battalions (National Mission for Clean Ganga) is also under consideration.

Who is eligible to apply

8. Inasmuch as the substantial challenge in this case is with regard to the prohibition of women candidates from joining the TA imposed by way of the advertisements being issued inviting application for joining, it becomes necessary to examine the prescriptions made by the respondents with regard to the eligibility based on gender and as prescribed by law.

9. Interestingly, the Brochure/handout furnished to the petitioner by the respondents, referred to above, contains no such prohibition either by gender or by unit. This handout gives information on "How to Join Territorial Army" as an officer. In the description of the process, it is stated that "gainfully employed civilians", who fulfilled the prescribed criteria being graduates between 18 to 42 years, can apply in response to advertisements published in leading national newspapers and the Employment News in May-June for civil candidates and December - January for ex officers each year.

10. The cause of action for filing the writ petition is premised on a

notice inviting the applications by way of the public advertisement, which is placed as Annexure-P1 to the writ petition. By way of this notice, the respondents invited applications captioned to "Join Territorial Army As An Officer".

11. We extract the relevant portion this notice inviting applications hereafter :

"JOIN TERRITORIAL ARMY

AS AN OFFICER

Applications are invited from gainfully employed young men for an opportunity of donning the uniform and serving the nation as Territorial Army Officers, based on the concept of enabling motivated young men to serve in a military environment without having to sacrifice their primary professions. You can serve the nation in two capacities - as a civilian and as a soldier. No other option allows you such an expanse of experiences.

PART TIME COMMITMENT - FULL TIME HONOUR : ADVENTURE AWAITS YOU!

ELIGIBILITY CONDITIONS
- *Only male citizens of India* and *Ex-service officers who are medically fit.*
- *Age* – *18 to 42 years as on* **30 Jun 2015.**
- *Qualification* – *Graduate from any recognized university.*
- *Employment* – *Gainfully Employed in Central/State Govt/Semi Govt/Pvt Sector/Self Employed.*
- *xxx*   *xxx*   *xxx*

- *Date of written Exam* : **02 Aug 2015**
  xxx   *xxx*   *xxx*"

As per this advertisement, there was thus an unequivocal and clear prohibition to women from applying for joining the TA.

12. An identical advertisement came to be issued by the respondents prescribing the last date of the application as 20th of June 2016 and

notifying the date of the written examination as 13th July, 2016. We have been informed by Ms. Charu Wali Khanna, ld. counsel for the petitioner that during the pendency of the writ petition itself, the respondents have issued identical advertisements repeatedly and completed several rounds of recruitment to the TA.

13. Appalled by this prohibition, the petitioner addressed a letter dated 8th August, 2015 to the Additional Directorate General of TA pointing out the illegality in the ouster of women from joining the TA as an officer, requesting an examination of the matter and a change in the policy which discriminated against women and to recruit women also along with the men in TA.

14. The response dated 8th September, 2015 of the respondents was emphatic, notifying the petitioner as follows :

"2. ..."as per para 6 of Appendix I of Territorial Army Act 1948 (Revised Edition 1976), woman are not eligible for Territorial Army so far."

(Emphasis by us)

15. So far as para 6 of Appendix I is concerned, the petitioner has placed the same before us. Appendix I is actually the Territorial Army Act, 1948 and reference to para 6 is in fact to Section 6 of the statute which reads as follows :

"6. Person eligible for enrolment - Any person who is a citizen of India may offer himself for enrolment in the Territorial Army, and may, if he satisfies the prescribed conditions, be enrolled for such period and subject to such conditions as may be prescribed."

(Emphasis by us)

16. The petitioner appears to have also addressed a query dated 29th April, 2016 under the Right to Information Act, 2005 to the respondents. In response to the petitioner's query seeking eligibility criteria for TA for female candidates, the following information had been furnished by the CPIO, Indian Army :

"xxx	xxx	xxx
(h)	*Kindly provide the eligibility criteria for Territorial Army for female candidate.*	**Female candidates are entitled** *for* **enrolment/commissioning** <u>**only in**</u> <u>**departmental TA units.**</u> *The* <u>**criteria**</u> *is as under :-* *(i) Age – 18 – 42 years.* *(ii) Medical Category – SHAPE-I* *(iii) Education Qualification –* *(aa) Officers – Graduation* *(ab) PBOR* *Matriculation with 45% marks.* *(iv) The candidate should also possess requisite technical qualification and should be recommended by the parent department.*
xxx	xxx	xxx "

(Emphasis by us)

Thus, as per this response, the prohibition to appointment of women to the TA is only with regard to infantry (non-departmental TA) units.

17. The respondents have also provided for grant of honorary commissions to industrialists, politicians and eminent personalities, as mentioned by the petitioner. This admission is contained in the counter affidavit. The respondents have stated that these honorary commissions are provided under the provisions of Para 31 of the Regulations for the Indian Territorial Army which states that "High Government officials, officers of the Army, Air Force and Navy and private gentlemen of good social position may be granted honorary commissions in the Territorial Army upto the rank of 'brigadier' by the Central Government". It is further stated that "the purpose of granting honorary rank to an individual, is to recognize his service of high order to the Union of India".

Thus grant of honorary commissions under para 31 of the Regulations for the Indian Territorial Army was also restricted to "gentlemen".

114

18. The respondents have placed before us a Corrigendum dated 22nd April, 2013 to the Territorial Army Regulation, 1948 (revised edition 1976) to para 31 by way of SRO 22 which shows that the restriction of grant of honorary commission to "gentlemen of good social position" was amended to read as "persons (which term shall include both men and women) of good social position". This amendment clearly shows that a conscious decision was taken by the Indian Territorial Army Directorate to amend the policy to enable both men and women occupying high social position to be granted honorary commissions.

19. In the counter affidavit filed on record, an effort has been made to explain the prohibition contained in the aforenoticed advertisement (Annexure P1). In para 3 of the preliminary submissions, the respondents have stated that "women can join and serve in Territorial Army in its Railway Engineer Regiments which is in consonance with existing policies of Govt. of India".

20. This assertion is sought to be supported by the communication dated 2nd July, 1997 addressed by the Ministry of Defence, Government of India to the Chief of the Army Staff on the subject of induction of women into Railway Engineers Regiment (TA). This communication clearly notifies the Chief of Army Staff regarding the sanction accorded by the President of India for "Commissioning/ enrolling women into Railway Engineer Regiment (TA) amongst the women employees of the Department of Railways who volunteer to serve in the Departmental Units of the Territorial Army and are within the age group of 18 years to 42 years".

21. So far as the postings of such women is concerned, we extract hereunder para 3 of this communication dated 9th of July 1997 which reads as follows :

"3. The women so commissioned/enrolled will only be appointed to work in posts tenable by the TA Component of the Departmental Territorial Army unit and will be granted rank/appointment in accordance with the rules governing the grant of such rank/ appointment to personnel enrolled in the Territorial Army."

(Emphasis supplied)

115

22. So far as the explanation for the prohibition contained in the impugned Advertisement is concerned, the respondents have sought to explain the same in para 3 of the counter affidavit stating that the extracted prohibition "was published for grant of commission in infantry units of ITA". It is further stated in the counter affidavit that "as on date commissioning in fighting arms in Indian Army, which comprises of Regular Army, Army reserves and Territorial Army, is restricted only to male citizens of India, and hence, the word 'male candidates' was specified in the advertisement." It has further been stated in para 4 of the counter affidavit that "women in ITA are not only granted commission as an officer in Railway Engineer Regiment as Engineer Officers, AMC officers, but are also permitted to seek enrolment as Other Ranks which, on date, is not allowed even in Regular Army/Indian Air Force/Indian Navy."

23. In the preliminary submissions made in the counter affidavit, the respondents have denied the petitioner's contention, that there was no scope for women to join the TA, as being factually incorrect.

24. So far as the entitlement for women to join the TA is concerned, it is stated that the respondents have however, restricted the eligibility of women to get commissioned in the Indian Territorial Army only into its Railway Engineer Regiments, as AMC officers and enrollment in other ranks which, according to them in consonance with the "existing policies of the Government of India". It is therefore, the clear stand of the government in the counter affidavit that women are not recruited into certain areas of the TA.

Judicial recognition of the greater role of women in all spheres of life

25. The prohibition to the recruitment of women in the present case is not the first instance of such a prohibition. Mr. Gautam Narayan, ld. amicus curiae has undertaken a careful analysis of prohibitions contained in the rules and policies of several statutory and non-statutory authorities and placed an outcome of the challenges to such discriminatory practices. We propose to briefly consider the same hereafter before we undertake an examination of the fact situation in the present case.

26. In the oft-cited judgment reported at MANU/SC/0580/1979 :

(1979) 4 SCC 260, C.B. Muthamma, I.F.S. v. Union of India & Ors., a challenge was laid by a senior member of the Indian Foreign Services complaining of hostile discrimination against women in the service. Rule 8 of the Indian Foreign Service (Conduct and Discipline) Rules, 1961 which required a woman member of the service to mandatorily obtain permission of the government, in writing, before her marriage was solemnized was assailed by the petitioner. This rule also prescribed that any time after the marriage, "a woman member of the service may be required to resign from service", if the government was satisfied that her family and domestic commitments are likely to come in the way of the due and efficient discharge of her duties as a member of the service. On the petitioner's challenge to this rule as being violative of Articles 14 and 16 of the Constitution of India, the Supreme Court, in the judgment penned by Krishna Iyer, J. for the Bench, observed as follows :

"6. At the first blush this rule is in defiance of Article 16. If a married man has a right, a married woman, other things being equal, stands on no worse footing. This misogynous posture is a hangover of the masculine culture of manacling the weaker sex forgetting how our struggle for national freedom was also a battle against woman's thraldom. Freedom is indivisible, so is Justice. That our founding faith enshrined in Articles 14 and 16 should have been tragically ignored vis-à-vis half of India's humanity viz. our women, is a sad reflection on the distance between Constitution in the book and law in action. And if the executive as the surrogate of Parliament, makes rules in the teeth of Part III especially when high political office, even diplomatic assignment has been filled by women, the inference of diehard allergy to gender parity is inevitable."

7. We do not mean to universalise or dogmatise that men and women are equal in all occupations and all situations and do not exclude the need to pragmatise where the requirements of particular employment, the sensitivities of sex or the peculiarities of societal sectors or the handicaps of either sex may compel selectivity. But save where the differentiation is demonstrable, the rule of equality must govern. ..."

(Emphasis by us)

27. In the pronouncement reported at MANU/SC/8173/2007 : (2008) 3 SCC 1, Anuj Garg & Ors. v. Hotel Association of India & Ors., the Supreme Court was concerned with a challenge to the Constitutional validity of Section 30 of the Punjab Excise Act, 1914 which prohibited employment of "any man under the age of 25 years" or "any woman" in any part of such premises in which liquor or intoxicating drugs were consumed by the public. The challenge had commenced by way of a writ petition, filed under Article 226 of the Constitution of India before a Division Bench of this court, in which the court had declared the statutory provision as ultra vires Articles 19(1)(g), 14 and 15 of the Constitution of India to the extent that it prohibited employment of any woman in any part of such premises, in which liquor or intoxicating drugs were consumed by the public. The decision was challenged before the Supreme Court, which, while repelling the challenge, upheld the judgment holding that prohibition from employment avenues in bars etc. was oppressive and violated the rights of the women. Some observations of the court which may have a bearing on the consideration in the present case deserve to be extracted in extenso and read thus :

"26. When a discrimination is sought to be made on the purported ground of classification, such classification must be founded on a rational criteria. The criteria which in absence of any constitutional provision and, it will bear repetition to state, having regard to the societal conditions as they prevailed in early 20th century, may not be a rational criteria in the 21st century. In the early 20th century, the hospitality sector was not open to women in general. In the last 60 years, women in India have gained entry in all spheres of public life. They have also been representing people at grassroot democracy. They are now employed as drivers of heavy transport vehicles, conductors of service carriages, pilots, et. al. Women can be seen to be occupying Class IV posts to the post of a Chief Executive Officer of a multinational company. They are now widely accepted both in police as also army services.

xxx xxx xxx

Right to employment vis-à-vis security : competing values

118

33. The instant matter involves a fundamental tension between right to employment and security.

34. The fundamental tension between autonomy and security is difficult to resolve. It is also a tricky jurisprudential issue. Right to self-determination is an important offshoot of gender justice discourse. At the same time, security and protection to carry out such choice or option specifically, and state of violence-free being generally is another tenet of the same movement. In fact, the latter is apparently a more basic value in comparison to right to options in the feminist matrix.

35. Privacy rights prescribe autonomy to choose profession whereas security concerns texture methodology of delivery of this assurance. But it is a reasonable proposition that the measures to safeguard such a guarantee of autonomy should not be so strong that the essence of the guarantee is lost. State protection must not translate into censorship.

36. At the same time we do not intend to further the rhetoric of empty rights. Women would be as vulnerable without State protection as by the loss of freedom because of the impugned Act. The present law ends up victimising its subject in the name of protection. In that regard the interference prescribed by the State for pursuing the ends of protection should be proportionate to the legitimate aims. The standard for judging the proportionality should be a standard capable of being called reasonable in a modern democratic society.

37. Instead of putting curbs on women's freedom, empowerment would be a more tenable and socially wise approach. This empowerment should reflect in the law enforcement strategies of the State as well as law modelling done in this behalf.

38. Also with the advent of modern State, new models of security must be developed. There can be a setting where the cost of security in the establishment can be distributed between the State and the employer.

(Emphasis by us)

28. Interestingly, the court also considered the stereotypes and

cultural norms and the requirement of deeper judicial scrutiny in paras 41 and 42 in following terms :

"Stereotype roles and right to options

41. Professor Williams in The Equality Crisis: Some Reflections on Culture, Courts and Feminism published in 7 Women's Rts. L. Rep., 175 (1982) notes issues arising where biological distinction between sexes is assessed in the backdrop of cultural norms and stereotypes. She characterises them as "hard cases". In hard cases, the issue of biological difference between sexes gathers an overtone of societal conditions so much so that the real differences are pronounced by the oppressive cultural norms of the time. This combination of biological and social determinants may find expression in popular legislative mandate. Such legislations definitely deserve deeper judicial scrutiny. It is for the court to review that the majoritarian impulses rooted in moralistic tradition do not impinge upon individual autonomy. This is the backdrop of deeper judicial scrutiny of such legislations world over.

42. Therefore, one issue of immediate relevance in such cases is the effect of the traditional cultural norms as also the state of general ambience in the society which women have to face while opting for an employment which is otherwise completely innocuous for the male counterpart. In such circumstances the question revolves around the approach of the State."

(Emphasis by us)

29. So far as the standard of judicial scrutiny is concerned, the Supreme Court observed as follows :

"The standard of judicial scrutiny

46. It is to be borne in mind that legislations with pronounced "protective discrimination" aims, such as this one, potentially serve as double-edged swords. Strict scrutiny test should be employed while assessing the implications of this variety of legislations. Legislation should not be only assessed on its proposed aims but rather on the implications and the effects. The impugned legislation suffers from incurable fixations of stereotype morality and conception of sexual

role. The perspective thus arrived at is outmoded in content and stifling in means.

47. No law in its ultimate effect should end up perpetuating the oppression of women. Personal freedom is a fundamental tenet which cannot be compromised in the name of expediency until and unless there is a compelling State purpose. Heighten ed level of scrutiny is the normative threshold for judicial review in such cases.

xxx xxx xxx

50. The test to review such a protective discrimination statute would entail a two-pronged scrutiny:

(a) the legislative interference (induced by sex discriminatory legalisation in the instant case) should be justified in principle,

(b) the same should be proportionate in measure.

51. The court's task is to determine whether the measures furthered by the State in the form of legislative mandate, to augment the legitimate aim of protecting the interests of women are proportionate to the other bulk of well-settled gender norms such as autonomy, equality of opportunity, right to privacy, et al. The bottom line in this behalf would be a functioning modern democratic society which ensures freedom to pursue varied opportunities and options without discriminating on the basis of sex, race, caste or any other like basis. In fine, there should be a reasonable relationship of proportionality between the means used and the aim pursued."

(Emphasis by us)

In conclusion, the Supreme Court held that the impact of the impugned Section 30 resulted in an invidious discrimination perpetrating sexual differences and upheld the judgment of this court.

30. Interestingly, before us the respondents have not even espoused the oft-used excuse of "protection" for the prohibition for recruitment of women to the TA.

31. Certain practices in the Air Force and Army were the subject of

contests before this court, which were dealt by way of a judgment dated 12th March, 2010 rendered in W.P.(C) No. 1597/2003 Babita Puniya v. The Secretary & Anr. and connected writ petitions which came to be reported at (2010) 168 DLT 115 (DB). In this judgment, this court had ruled on a challenge to the denial of permanent commission only to women officers, who were commissioned into the Air Force and the Army in the Short Service Commission. The court had, inter alia, observed that the women officials had undertaken the same training of one year as the male permanent commissioned officers whereas 10 batches of male short commissioned officers who had undergone training of much lesser period, of only three months, in the Air Force Administrative College were considered and granted permanent commission in the same period, when women short service commissioned officers continued to work in that capacity. So far as the areas of operation of Air Force where women should be employed was concerned, the court observed that it being a policy decision, this was an issue which was not for the court to decide. Furthermore, it was observed that the policy decision not to offer permanent commission to Short Service Commissioned officers across the board for men and women being on parity and as part of manpower management exercises, was a policy decision which was not required to be interfered with. The court however, observed that the questions of suitability or requirement were not in doubt and that the advertisement issued by the respondents held out a promise to women Air Force officers for grant of permanent commission depending on two factors which were vacancy, position and suitability of the officer. The officers had thus joined the Air Force on the promise of these terms of recruitment apart from other conditions of service and the respondents could not introduce an alien element other than these two elements. It therefore, ruled that the Short Service Commissioned officers of the Air Force who had opted for permanent commission and were not granted permanent commission but granted extension of Short Service Commissions, as well as those of the Army, were entitled to permanent commission at par with male Short Service Commissioned officers with all consequential benefits.

32. In the judgment reported at MANU/SC/1044/2014 : (2015)

1 SCC 192, Charu Khurana & Ors. v. Union of India & Ors., the Supreme Court was concerned with gender discrimination in the film industry. The Cine Costume Make-Up Artists and Hair Dressers Association in Maharashtra had made bye-laws prohibiting women to work as make-up artists and only permitting them to work as hair dressers. The petitioner, who was a trained make-up artist and hair stylist, was rejected a membership card as a make-up artist resulting in the challenge. In this seminal decision of the Supreme Court, it was held that prohibiting women from working as make-up artists offended Articles 14, 15, 19(1)(g) and 21 of the Constitution of India. The court held as follows :

"52. Thus, the aforesaid decision in Vishaka case [Vishaka v. State of Rajasthan, MANU/SC/0786/1997 : (1997) 6 SCC 241 : 1997 SCC (Cri) 932] unequivocally recognises gender equality as a fundamental right. The discrimination done by the Association, a trade union registered under the Act, whose rules have been accepted, cannot take the route of the discrimination solely on the basis of sex. It really plays foul of the statutory provisions. It is absolutely violative of constitutional values and norms. If a female artist does not get an opportunity to enter into the arena of being a member of the Association, she cannot work as a female artist. It is inconceivable. The likes of the petitioners are given membership as hair dressers, but not as make-up artist. There is no fathomable reason for the same. It is gender bias writ large. It is totally impermissible and wholly unacceptable."

33. The court finally concluded as follows :

"57. It is really shocking that Respondent 5 has maintained such an adamantine attitude. In ordinary circumstances, the Registrar would have been directed to cancel the registration but we do not intend to do so. As the clauses relating to the membership and the domicile, namely, Clauses 4 and 6, are violative of the statutory provisions and the constitutional mandate and taking further note of the fact that the Registrar would have been, in normal circumstances, directed by us requiring the trade union to delete the clauses, we quash the said clauses and further direct that the petitioners shall be registered as members of the fifth respondent within four weeks. It will be the obligation of the Registrar of Trade Unions to see that they are registered as make-up artists. If the Association would create any hurdle, it will be obligatory on the part of the police administration to see that the female make-up artists are not harassed in any manner whatsoever, for harassment of a woman is absolutely unconscionable, unacceptable and intolerable. Our directions close the matter as far as the State of Maharashtra is concerned."

(Emphasis by us)

34. Lastly, our attention is drawn to the pronouncement dated 4th September, 2015 in W.P.(C) No. 7336/2010, Annie Nagaraja & Ors. v. Union of India & Ors. and connected writ petitions, reported at MANU/DE/2573/2015, whereby this court decided six writ petitions filed by 70 women officers who had joined Indian Navy as Short Service Commissioned officers in different branches which includes Education, Logistics and ATC seeking entitlement to permanent commission. In para 32 of the judgment, the court noted that the petitioners along with male officers had undertaken the same kind of training but nevertheless were denied permanent commission although the men were granted the permanent commission with no special merit except for the fact that they were males. It was held that this tantamounted to gender discrimination. The court held that the 2008 policy of the respondents which took no care to offer permanent commission to the women officers in the branches where these officers had worked as Short Service Commissioned officers for 14 years, was irrational and a clear case of discrimination and granted relief to the petitioners.

35. Article 14 of the Constitution of India provides that the State shall not deny to any person equality before the law or equal protection of laws within the territory of India. The State is precluded from discriminating against any citizens on grounds only of religion, caste, sex, place or any of them under Article 15(1). Article 16 embodies the fundamental guarantee that there shall be equality of opportunity for all citizens in matters relating to employment or appointment to any office under the State.

36. We may usefully refer to, what, Lord Denning, in his book "Due

Process of Law", has observed about women in the following words:

"A woman feels as keenly, thinks as clearly, as a man. She in her sphere does work as useful as man does in his. She has as much right to her freedom - to develop her personality to the full as a man. When she marries, she does not become the husband's servant but his equal partner. If his work is more important in life of the community, her's is more important of the family. Neither can do without the other. Neither is above the other or under the other. They are equals."

37. The aforenoticed judicial pronouncements effectuate these values and rights.

38. In this regard, useful reference may also be made to the pronouncement of the Supreme Court reported at MANU/SC/0458/2003 : (2003) 6 SCC 277 Air India Cabin Crew Assn. v. Yeshaswinee Merchant & Ors in the following terms:

"39. Article 14 of the Constitution mandates that the State shall not deny to any person equality before the law or the equal protection of the laws within the territory of India. Clauses (1) and (2) of Article 15 prohibit the State from discriminating any citizen on grounds only of religion, race, caste, sex, place of birth or any of them. Article 16 which contains the fundamental right of equality of opportunity in matters of public employment, by sub-clause (2) thereof guarantees that:

"16. (2) No citizen shall, on grounds only of religion, race, caste, sex, descent, place of birth, residence or any of them, be ineligible for, or discriminated against in respect of, any employment or office under the State."

40. Article 16(2) prohibits discrimination only on sex but clause (3) of Article 15 enables the State to make "any special provision for women and children". Articles 15 and 16 read together prohibit direct discrimination between members of different sexes if they would have received the same treatment as comparable to members of the opposite gender. The two Articles do not prohibit special treatment of women. The constitutional mandate is infringed only where the females would have received same treatment with males

125

but for their sex.

41. In English law "but-for-sex" test has been developed to mean that no less favourable treatment is to be given to women on gender-based criterion which would favour the opposite sex and women will not be deliberately selected for less favourable treatment because of their sex..."

(Emphasis supplied)

39. The established principles governing Articles 14, 15 and 16 came be to succinctly summarized by the Supreme Court in the pronouncement reported at MANU/SC/0755/2003 : (2003) 8 SCC 440 Vijay Lakshmi v. Punjab University as follows:

"4. ...we would refer to established propositions of law interpreting Articles 14 to 16, which are:

• Article 14 does not bar rational classification.

• Reasonable discrimination between female and male for an object sought to be achieved is permissible.

• Question of unequal treatment does not arise if there are different sets of circumstances.

• Equality of opportunity for unequals can only mean aggravation of inequality.

• Equality of opportunity admits discrimination with reasons and prohibits discrimination without reason. Discrimination with reasons means rational classification for differential treatment having nexus with constitutionally permissible objects. It is now an accepted jurisprudence and practice that the concept of equality before the law and the prohibition of certain kinds of discrimination do not require identical treatment. Equality means the relative equality, namely, the principle to treat equally what are equal and unequally what are unequal. To treat unequals differently according to their inequality is not only permitted but required (Re St. Stephen's College v. University of Delhi[MANU/SC/0319/1992 : (1992) 1 SCC 558].)

• Sex is a sound basis for classification.

• Article 15(3) categorically empowers the State to make special provision for women and children.

• Articles 14, 15 and 16 are to be read conjointly."

40. Therefore it emerges that the state may be empowered to discriminate reasonably, provided such discrimination is for an object which is sought to be achieved.

41. The writ petitioner relies also on Article 39(a) in Part IV of the Constitution of India dealing with the Directive Principles of State Policy which provides that the State shall direct its policies towards securing the citizens, men and women equally, for their rights to adequate means of livelihood.

42. We may notice the landmark pronouncement reported at MANU/SC/0380/1973 : AIR 1974 SC 555, E.P. Royappa v. State of Tamil Nadu & Anr. wherein it was held by Bhagwati, J., in his separate but concurring view, thus :

"85. ... Article 16 embodies the fundamental guarantee that there shall be equality of opportunity for all citizens in matters relating to employment or appointment to any office under the State. Though enacted as a distinct and independent fundamental right because of its great importance as a principle ensuring equality of opportunity in public employment which is so vital to the building up of the new classless egalitarian society envisaged in the Constitution, Article 16 is only an instance of the application of the concept of equality enshrined in Article 14. In other words, Article 14 is the genus while Article 16 is a species. Article 16 gives effect to the doctrine of equality in all matters relating to public employment. The basic principle which, therefore, informs both Articles 14 and 16 is equality and inhibition against discrimination. Now, what is the content and reach of this great equalising principle? It is a founding faith, to use the words of Bose. J., "a way of life", and it must not be subjected to a narrow pedantic or lexicographic approach. We cannot countenance any attempt to truncate its all-embracing scope and meaning, for to do so would be to violate its activist magnitude. Equality is a dynamic concept with many aspects and dimensions and it cannot be "cribbed, cabined and confined" within traditional and doctrinaire limits. From a positivistic point of view, equality is antithetic to arbitrariness. In fact equality and arbitrariness are sworn enemies; one belongs to the rule of law in a republic while the other, to the whim and caprice of an absolute monarch. Where an act is arbitrary, it is implicit in it that it is unequal both according to political logic and constitutional law and is therefore violative of Article 14, and if it effects any matter relating to public employment, it is also violative of Article 16. Articles 14 and 16 strike at arbitrariness in State action and ensure fairness and equality of treatment. They require that State action must be based on valid relevant principles applicable alike to all similarly situate and it must not be guided by any extraneous or irrelevant considerations because that would be denial of equality. ..."

(Emphasis by us)

43. The writ petitioner, has also contended that the discrimination being complained of also borders on human rights violation. In this respect, we may refer to the pronouncement of the Supreme Court reported at MANU/SC/0275/1996 : (1996) 3 SCC 545, Valsamma Paul (Mrs) v. Cochin University where it was remarked that "... All forms of discrimination on grounds of gender is violative of fundamental freedoms and human rights..."

44. The challenge before us has to be examined in the light of these well settled principles.

The respondent's stand that the prohibition was as per the extant policy which was as per the Territorial Army Act, 1948

45. As noted above, in the response dated 8th of September 2015 to the petition, the respondents had informed the petitioner that the present policy was as per para 6 (i.e. Section 6 of the Territorial Army Act, 1948). This position stands reiterated in the counter affidavit. The respondents have further stated that amendment in this policy would require an amendment in the Act itself. It therefore, becomes necessary to examine the statutory position as to whether there is actually any statutory bar to the recruitment of women in the Territorial Army.

46. Mr. Gautam Narayan, Advocate, who appears as amicus curiae, has painstakingly taken us through the statutory scheme. It has been emphasized that the statutory interpretation must be in consonance with today's day and age given the fact that a period of more than almost 70 years have lapsed since the 1948 when the enactment was brought into force.

47. We have, with the assistance of Mr. Gautam Narayan, ld. amicus curiae, examined the statutory scheme. Section 6 of the said statute extracted above sets out the contentions for eligibility for enrollment. Section 6 clearly makes eligible any "person" who is a citizen of India. The respondents appear to be relying on the statutory reference to "he" in the later portion to the effect that "if he satisfies the prescribed conditions".

48. So far as interpretation of the expression "he" is concerned, reference has to be made to the provisions of Section 13 of the General Clauses Act, 1897 which reads thus :

"13 Gender and number. -In all Central Acts and Regulations, unless there is anything repugnant in the subject or context,-

(1) words importing the masculine gender shall be taken to include females; and

(2) words in the singular shall include the plural, and vice versa."

(Emphasis by us)

49. Clearly the use of expression "he" in the later part of Section 6 of the Territorial Army Act, 1948 has to be reasonably interpreted to include females. In the opening words, Section 6 uses the compendious expression "any person". It is important to note that the respondents do not suggest that there is anything repugnant to the context if such an interpretation is to be adopted.

50. The view we are taking is also supported by the unequivocal declaration made in the handout and brochure prepared and circulated by the respondents which includes any civilian can seek recruitment in the Indian Territorial Army.

51. At this stage, we may usefully also advert to following certain

provisions of Section 6A of the Territorial Army Act, 1948 which imposes liability upon certain persons to render compulsory service into the TA :

"6A. Liability of certain persons for compulsory service in the Territorial Army.-(1) Without prejudice to the provision contained in section 6, every person employed under the Government or in a public utility service who has attained the age of twenty years but has not completed the age of forty years shall, subject to the other provisions contained in this section and subject to such rules as may be made in this behalf, be liable, when so required to do, to perform service in the Territorial Army.

xxx xxx xxx

(4) Every person liable to perform service under subsection (1) shall, if so required by the prescribed authority, be bound to fill up such norms as may be prescribed and sign and lodge them with the prescribed authority within such time as may be specified in the requisition.

(5) The prescribed authority may require any person incharge of the management of a public utility service to furnish within such time as may be specified in the requisition such particulars as may be prescribed with respect to persons employed under him, who may be liable to perform service under sub-section (1)

xxx xxx xxx

Explanation.-For the purposes of this section, the expression "person employed under the Government or in a public utility service" shall not include-

(a) a woman;

xxx xxx xxx"

(Emphasis by us)

A plain reading of the above statutory provision manifests that the Legislature has consciously and expressly excluded women from inclusion within the ambit of the expression "person" by way of a specific explanation to the statutory provision.

52. The stand of the respondents that the policy of exclusion of women from seeking recruitment in all branches in the TA, is based on or informed by the provisions of Territorial Army Act, 1948, is therefore, clearly belied upon the complete reading of the statutory scheme, more specifically of Section 6, which contains no such exclusion. Unlike the specific exclusion of women from the application of Section 6A, there is clearly no prohibition at all under Section 6 of the statute which provides the eligibility of enrolment.

53. The above position is also manifested from the schemes of other legislations relating to the armed forces. Mr. Gautam Narayan, ld. amicus curiae has carefully drawn our attention to the statutory provisions governing the Indian Army, Air Force and Navy. We find that Section 12 of the Army Act, 1950; Section 12 of the Air Force Act, 1950 as well as Section 9 of the Indian Navy Act, 1957 contain specific and express provisions excluding women from eligibility for enrolment. In this regard, it may be useful to advert to these provisions of the statute which read thus :

The Army Act, 1950

"12. Ineligibility of females for enrolment or employment. - No female shall be eligible for enrolment or employment in the regular Army, except in such corps, department, branch or other body forming part of, or attached to any portion of, the regular Army as the Central Government may, by notification in the Official Gazette, specify in this behalf:

Provided that nothing contained in this section shall affect the provisions of any law for the time being in force providing for the raising and maintenance of any service auxiliary to the regular Army, or any branch thereof in which females are eligible for enrolment or employment."

The Air Force Act, 1950

"12. Ineligibility of females for enrolment or employment.-No female shall be eligible for enrolment or employment in the Air Force, except in such corps, department, branch or other body forming part of, or attached to any portion of, the Air Force as the Central Government may, by notification, specify in this behalf:

Provided that nothing contained in this section shall affect the provisions of any law for the time being in force providing for the raising and maintenance of any service auxiliary to the Air Force or any branch thereof in which females are eligible for enrolment or employment"

The Navy Act, 1957

"9. Eligibility for appointment or enrolment.-(1) No person who is not a citizen of India shall be eligible for appointment or enrolment in the Indian Navy or the Indian Naval Reserve Forces except with the consent of the Central Government.

Provided that nothing in this section shall render a person ineligible for appointment or enrolment in the Indian Navy or the Indian Naval Reserve Forces on the ground that he is a subject of Nepal.

(2) No woman shall be eligible for appointment or enrolment in the Indian Navy or the Indian Naval Reserve Forces except in such department, branch or other body forming part thereof or attached thereto and subject to such conditions as the Central Government may, by notification in the Official Gazette, specify in this behalf."

54. Clearly, the stand of the respondents, reading an implied bar into the statute justifying an extant policy of exclusion, is premised on misreading of Section 6 of the Territorial Army Act and has to be rejected.

Whether the advertisement invites applications only to infantry units of the TA?

55. The respondents have pressed the stand in the counter affidavit and before us that the impugned advertisement is confined to recruitment to infantry units of the TA. As discussed above, a bare reading of the Act suggests that there is no bar to recruitment of women in departmental units.

56. We have extracted the relevant provisions of the advertisement above. It nowhere states that the applications are invited for

recruitment only to infantry units of the TA. There is no clarification at all in the advertisement that women may seek recruitment to departmental units of the TA. Therefore, the stand taken in the counter affidavit and in the oral submissions by Mr. Amit Mahajan, Central Government Standing Counsel for the Union of India - respondent No. 1, that the advertisement relates only to infantry units of the TA is contrary to the document. The advertisement invites applications to all battalions of the Territorial Army and imposes an absolute prohibition to the commissioning and recruitment of women into it.

Whether there is any rationale or basis to justify the prohibition for recruitment/enrolment/commissioning of women?

57. The issue of the prohibition for commissioning of women into the non-departmental units can be examined through yet another pertinent aspect, which has been also placed before us. As noted above, no differentiation or basis for justifying the prohibition has been placed before us.

58. So far as the differentiation in the job requirements of the departmental battalions and non-departmental battalions are concerned, even the job profile of the battalions has not been placed before us. However, we have before us the prescription of the training, which a candidate has to undergo upon enrolment.

After setting out the eligibility conditions, the impugned advertisement itself contains the details of the training which a candidate has to undergo and prescribes as follows :

"xxx xxx xxx
EMBODIMENT FOR TRAINING
• *One month basic training in the first year of commission.*
• *Two months annual training camp every year including the first year.*
• *Three months Post Commissioning training within first two years at IMA Dehradun.*
• *Date of written Exam :* **02 Aug 2015**
xxx xxx xxx"

(Emphasis by us)

133

Therefore, not only does the advertisement not draw any distinction between applications for departmental and non-departmental battalions but it also does not prescribes different eligibility conditions nor any differentiation even in the training which is imparted to all candidates, male or female. The discrimination against entry of women into the Territorial Army is also not supported by the training regime.

Submission that exclusion of women from roles in the Territorial Army is irrational

59. The respondents have placed no material at all to support the prohibition for not appointing women in the non-departmental battalions. There is not an iota of empirical or statistical data or any scientific study or analysis produced by the respondents to justify such policy prohibiting partial recruitment of women as per the counter affidavit, or, the total prohibition as manifested by the impugned advertisement.

60. An extensive research appears to have been undertaken by Mr. Gautam Narayan, ld. amicus curiae which deserves to be noticed. The ld. amicus curiae has placed before us a study undertaken by the Canadian Armed Forces being the "SWINTER Trials" (an acronym for "Service Women In Non Traditional Environment and Roles") for a five year period between 1980-84 with the object of collecting verifiable and quantifiable data to ascertain problems (physical, psychological and social) that might arise if all military operations were open to women without any restrictions. The study also attempted to ascertain as to whether the operational effectiveness of the armed forces would be affected, if women were to be recruited. After a detailed analysis and assessment, eventually in the year 1989, Canada allowed women to be recruited in combat roles.

61. In support of the submission that the recruitment of women in combat roles does not actually impact operational effectiveness of the armed forces, Mr. Gautam Narayan, ld. amicus curiae has placed the following tabulation of countries which allow women to serve even in combat roles in its defence forces, along with the year from which they were so allowed :

"Sr.No.	Countries	Year from which women were allowed in combat roles
(i)	North Korea	1950
(ii)	Netherlands	1979
(iii)	Sweden	1989
(iv)	Canada	1989
(v)	Denmark	1988
(vi)	Norway	1985
(vii)	Spain	1999
(viii)	Eritrea	1998
(ix)	France	1998
(x)	Israel	1995
(xi)	Finland	1994
(xii)	Lithuania	2000
(xiii)	Germany	2000
(xiv)	New Zealand	2001
(xv)	Romania	2002
(xvi)	Poland	2004
(xvii)	Australia	2011

62. So far as the armed forces in India are concerned, our attention is drawn to a news report dated 21st November, 2017 titled "SALUTE TO THE INDIAN SOLDIER" which refers to three women becoming fighter pilots in the Indian Air Force.

63. Given our finding that the stand in the counter affidavit and action of the respondents in imposing the prohibition against entry of women into the Territorial Army by way of the impugned advertisements have no statutory support, has no factual basis at all and is irrational, it is not necessary for us to deal with the issue as to whether prohibition of engagement in the combat roles would be justified or not.

Development of the law in other jurisdictions

64. A careful evaluation of the military service of women in other jurisdictions has been placed by Mr. Gautam Narayan, amicus curiae before us which manifests that more and more countries have moved away from positions of total prohibition/exclusion of women to permitting recruitment of women even in combat roles in the Armed Forces. The tabulation extracted above would show that approximately 22 countries permit recruitment of women even in

combat roles.

65. In the pronouncement by the Supreme Court of the United States reported at MANU/USSC/0215/1981 : 453 US 57 (1981), Rostker v. Goldberg, the court was considering the challenge to the Military Selective Service Act which required registration for possible military service of males but not females, the purpose of the registration being to facilitate any eventual conscription under the Act. In 1980, the President of the United States of America had recommended that the Congress amend the Act to permit the registration and conscription of women as well as men. The Parliament declined to amend the Act to permit registration of women. A lawsuit was brought by several men challenging the Act's constitutionality. The three-judge District Court ultimately held that the Act's gender based discrimination violated the "Due Process Clause" of the Fifth Amendment and enjoined registration under the Act. The opinion of the court was delivered by Rehnquist, J., in which Burger, C.J., and Stewart, Blackmun, Powell and Stevens, JJ. joined. White, J. and Marshall, J., filed dissenting opinions, in which, Brennan, J., joined. It was held by the majority that the Congress had acted well within its Constitutional authority when it authorized the registration of men and not women under the Military Selective Service Act and that non-registration of women for possible military service under the enactment was not violative of the Fifth Amendment.

66. In yet another determinative decision reported at MANU/USSC/0073/1996 : 518 US 515 (1996), United States v. Virginia et al., the United States Supreme Court was considering the decision rendered by the Court of Appeals for the Fourth Circuit laying down that the exclusion of women from the educational opportunities by the Virginia Military Institute (VMI) was violative of the equal protection to women. In 1990, prompted by a complaint filed with the Attorney General by a female high school student seeking admission to the Virginia Military Institute (VMI), the United States sued the Commonwealth of Virginia and VMI, alleging that VMI's exclusively male admission policy violated the Equal Protection Clause of the Fourteenth Amendment. The VMI was the sole single sex school amongst Virginia's public institutions of higher learning

with the mission of producing "Citizen-Soldiers", men prepared for leadership in civilian life and in military service. The District Court had ruled in VMI's favour. The Fourth Circuit reversed and ordered Virginia to remedy the Constitutional violation. In response, Virginia proposed a parallel program for women. The District Court found that Virginia's proposal satisfied the Constitution's equal protection requirement, and the Fourth Circuit affirmed. The appeals court deferentially reviewed Virginia's plan and determined that provision of single-gender educational options was a legitimate objective.

67. The opinion of the United States Supreme Court was delivered by Ginsburg, J. in which Stevens, O'Connor, Kennedy, Souter and Breyer, JJ. joined. Rehnquist, C.J., filed a concurring opinion while Scalia, J., filed a dissenting opinion. The Supreme Court considered its current directions for cases of official classification based on gender pointing out that the court must determine : (i) Whether the proffered justification is "exceedingly persuasive". The burden of justification is demanding and it rests entirely on the State; (ii) The State must show "at least that the challenged classification serves 'important governmental objectives and that the discriminatory means employed' are substantially related to the achievement of those objectives"; (iii) The justification must be genuine, not hypothesized or invented post hoc in response to litigation; (iv) It must not rely on overbroad generalizations about the different talents, capacities, or preferences of males and females.

It was held that Virginia has shown no "exceedingly persuasive justification" for excluding all women from the "Citizen-Soldiers" training afforded by the VMI.

68. In MANU/USSC/0165/1979 : 442 US 256 (1979) Personnel Administrator of Massachusetts v. B Feeney, the United States Supreme Court held as follows:

"22. ... Classifications based upon gender, not unlike those based upon race, have traditionally been the touchstone for pervasive and often subtle discrimination. Caban v. Mohammed, 441 U.S. 380, 398, 99 S.Ct. 1760, 1771, 60 L.Ed. 2d 297 (STEWART, J., dissenting). This Court's recent cases teach that such classifications must bear a close and substantial relationship to important governmental objectives... and are in many settings unconstitutional. Reed v. Reed, 404 U.S. 71, 92 S.Ct. 251, 30 L.Ed. 2d 225; Frontiero v. Richardson, 411 U.S. 677, 93 S.Ct. 1764, 36 L.Ed. 2d 583; Weinberger v. Wiesenfeld, 420 U.S. 636, 95 S.Ct. 1225, 43 L.Ed. 2d 514; Craig v. Boren, supra; Califano v. Goldfarb, 430 U.S. 199, 97 S.Ct. 1021, 51 L.Ed. 2d 270; Orr v. Orr, 440 U.S. 268, 99 S.Ct. 1102, 59 L.Ed. 2d 306; Caban v. Mohammed, supra. Although public employment is not a constitutional right, ... and the States have wide discretion in framing employee qualifications, ...these precedents dictate that any state law overtly or covertly designed to prefer males over females in public employment would require an exceedingly persuasive justification to withstand a constitutional challenge under the Equal Protection Clause of the Fourteenth Amendment."

(Emphasis by us)

69. In these terms, it is apposite to refer to another decision of the United States Supreme Court reported at 441 US 380 (1979) : 1979 SCC OnLine US SC 72 Caban v. Mohammed where ruling on gender based distinctions it was held thus:

"14. Gender-based distinctions "must serve important governmental objectives and must be substantially related to achievement of those objectives" in order to withstand judicial scrutiny under the Equal Protection Clause. Craig v. Boren, 429 U.S. 190, 197, 97 S.Ct. 451, 457, 50 L.Ed. 2d 397 (1976). See also Reed v. Reed, 404 U.S. 71, 92 S.Ct. 251, 30 L.Ed. 2d 225 (1971)..."

(Emphasis by us)

70. In a decision of the United States District Court for the District of Columbia reported at 455 F. Supp. 291 (D.D.C. 1978), Owens v. Brown, the court decided that the absolute prohibition that prevents the Secretary from exercising the discretion to assign female personnel to duty at sea is violation of the Fifth Amendment of the Constitution.

71. Mr. Gautam Narayan, amicus curiae has also placed a decision of the Supreme Court of Israel reported at HCJ 4541/94, Alice Miller

v. Minister of Defence which held that the budgetary and planning considerations did not justify a general policy of rejecting all women from being trained as Air Force pilots.

72. In a decision of the Court of Justice of the European Communities in case C-285/98, Kreil v. Germany, it was decided that on the implementation of the principle of equal treatment for men and women as regards access to employment, vocational training and promotion, and working conditions precludes the application of national provisions such as those of German law, which impose a general exclusion of women from military posts involving the use of arms and which allow them access only to the medical and military music services.

73. Yet another decision of the Court of Justice of European Communities in case C-273/97 reported at (1999) ECR I-7403, Angela Sirdar v. Army Board, has been placed before us by Mr. Gautam Narayan, amicus curiae. In this decision, the court upheld the exclusion of women from the Royal Marines to be justified by reason of the nature of activities in question and the context in which they were carried out.

74. In the decision reported at (1989) C.H.R.D. No. 3, Gauthier v. Canadian Armed Force, the Canadian Human Rights Tribunal held that there is no risk of failure of performance of combat duties by women sufficient to justify a general exclusionary policy in respect of their entry to the Canadian Armed Forces. A policy of this sort cannot constitute a bonafide constitutional requirement and is deemed to be discriminatory on the grounds of sex.

75. The above decisions would support the submissions made on behalf of the petitioner by Mr. Gautam Narayan, Advocate, appearing as amicus curiae as well as Dr. Charu Wali Khanna, Advocate that the prohibition in the advertisements as well as the claimed policy to deny recruitment to women in non-departmental units of the Territorial Army is based on no rationale and is completely unjustified and arbitrary.

Conclusion

76. Women are eligible for recruitment and appointment to the Territorial Army under Section 6 of the Indian Territorial Army Act, 1948.

77. The respondents have failed to show any decision of policy, let alone binding policy, enabling them to deny opportunity to the women to serve in all units of the TA. No rationale has been offered to justify or sustain the action of the respondents enforcing a bar against recruitment of women through their advertisements.

78. Even as per the Brochure printed and circulated by the respondents, all gainfully employed civilians, irrespective of their gender, who are graduates between 18 to 42 years are eligible for applying for consideration for appointment to the TA.

79. So far as the prohibition notified in the Advertisements with regard to employment of women is concerned, the same is not supported either by statute or by any policy document placed on record.

80. The impugned advertisements imposing a blanket bar on appointment of women to both departmental and non-departmental battalions of the TA without any credible, reasonable or compelling justification for imposing such restrictions. The restriction of enrolment of women contained in the impugned advertisements and the claimed policy is neither reasonable nor rational and has to be quashed.

Result

81. It is declared that 'any person' mentioned in Section 6 of the Territorial Army Act, 1948 includes both males as well as females.

82. The impugned advertisements to the extent they exclude women from appointment to the Territorial Army and the claimed policy in this regard are ultra vires of Articles 14, 15, 16 and 19(1)(g) of the Constitution of India and are hereby quashed.

83. The writ petition is allowed in the above terms.

84. We record our deep appreciation for Mr. Gautam Narayan, Amicus Curiae for the valuable assistance rendered to this court.

85. In view of the above, CM No. 44852/2016 does not survive for adjudication and is hereby disposed of.

Chapter -7

Conclusion

Equality cannot be achieved unless there are equal opportunities and if a woman is debarred at the threshold to enter in to the sphere of profession for which she is eligible and qualified, it is well-nigh impossible to conceive of equality. It also clips her capacity to earn her livelihood which affects her individual dignity.

A woman feels as keenly, thinks as clearly, as a man. She in her sphere does work as useful as man does in his. She has as much right to her freedom - to develop her personality to the full as a man. When she marries, she does not become the husband's servant but his equal partner. If his work is more important in life of the community, her's is more important of the family. Neither can do without the other. Neither is above the other or under the other. They are equals.[1] *Gender equality is more than a goal in itself. It is a precondition for meeting the challenge of reducing poverty, promoting sustainable development and building good governance.*[2]

Court held that so far as interpretation of the expression "he" is concerned, reference has to be made to the provisions of Section 13 of the General Clauses Act, 1897 which reads thus: "13 Gender and number. -In all Central Acts and Regulations, unless there is anything repugnant in the subject or context,- (1) words importing the masculine gender shall be taken to include females; and (2) words in the singular shall include the plural, and vice versa." Clearly the use of expression "he" in the later part of Section 6 of the Territorial Army Act, 1948 has to be reasonably interpreted to include females.

---

1   Lord Denning in his book "Due Process of Law", has observed about women.

2   Speech by U.N. Secretary General Kofi Annan.

Therefore, the stand of the respondents, reading an implied bar into the statute justifying an extant policy of exclusion, is premised on misreading of Section 6 of the Territorial Army Act and has to be rejected.

Court therefore held that women are eligible for recruitment and appointment to the Territorial Army under Section 6 of the Indian Territorial Army Act, 1948. The respondents have failed to show any decision of policy, let alone binding policy, enabling them to deny opportunity to the women to serve in all units of the TA. No rationale has been offered to justify or sustain the action of the respondents enforcing a bar against recruitment of women through their advertisements. Even as per the Brochure printed and circulated by the respondents, all gainfully employed civilians, irrespective of their gender, who are graduates between 18 to 42 years are eligible for applying for consideration for appointment to the TA. So far as the prohibition notified in the Advertisements with regard to employment of women was concerned, the same was not supported either by statute or by any policy document placed on record. The restriction of enrolment of women contained in the impugned advertisements and the claimed policy was neither reasonable nor rational was quashed by court.

Court held that 'any person' mentioned in Section 6 of the Territorial Army Act, 1948 includes both males as well as females. The impugned advertisements to the extent they exclude women from appointment to the Territorial Army and the claimed policy in this regard was ultra vires of Articles 14, 15, 16 and 19(1)(g) of the Constitution of India and was quashed.

In the last 75 years women in India have gained entry in all spheres of public life. They have also been representing people at grass root democracy. They are now employed as drivers of heavy transport vehicles, conductors of services carriage, pilots etc. All women can be seen to be occupying class IV posts, to the post of a Chief Executive Officer of a Multinational company and they are now widely accepted in both police and army services yet they face discrimination.

On the other hand, decision to marry and the age of marriage for girls in India continue to remain at hands of parents and their families. It is commonplace for girls pursuing their under-graduate/ graduate studies to be married off. Thereafter, pregnancy and child bearing are decisions which are often beyond their control and are influenced by family and social pressures. Therefore, rights of women who are focussed on obtaining higher education and making their careers despite such severe challenges ought to be protected.

The human rights for woman is inalienable and it is an integral and an indivisible part of human rights. The full development of personality and fundamental freedoms and equal participation by women in political, social, economic and cultural life are concomitants for national development and growth. All forms or dimensions of discrimination on ground of gender is violative of fundamental freedom and human rights.

Women Sexist bias and stereotypes seem to have dogged the service conditions of women serving in the Forces. The march of time has proven that gender does not define ability and or calibre. Equality cannot be achieved unless there are equal opportunities and if a woman is debarred at the threshold to enter into the sphere of profession for which she is eligible and qualified, it is well-nigh impossible to conceive of equality. It also clips her capacity to earn her livelihood which affects her individual dignity.

State has a duty to ensure that there is no discrimination practiced by anyone in the country and non recruitment of female candidates who are gainfully employed is against the spirit of the constitution. Non-recruitment of female candidates just because they are females by the Defence forces is a discrimination against the females only because they are females. In today's time, there is no scope for discrimination on the ground of gender, institutionalized discrimination at the hands of State is unimaginable. At various occasions, concerns have been raised against such discriminations and when the system failed to address these concerns, Judiciary was approached and Judiciary played a pivotal role in neutralizing the perpetual discrimination against females.

Annexure I (Year 2015)

JOIN TERRITORIAL ARMY
AS AN OFFICER

Applications are invited from gainfully employed young men for an opportunity of donning the uniform and serving the nation as Territorial Army Officers, based on the concept of enabling motivated young men to serve in a military environment without having to sacrifice their primary professions. You can serve the nation in two capacities – as a civilian and as a soldier. No other option allows you such an expanse of experiences.

PART TIME COMMITMENT – FULL TIME HONOUR : ADVENTURE AWAITS YOU !

ELIGIBILITY CONDITIONS
- Only male citizens of India and Ex-service officers who are medically fit.
- **Age**- 18 to 42 years as on 30 Jun 2015.
- **Qualification** -Graduate from any recognized university.
- **Employment** - Gainfully Employed in Central/State Govt/ Semi Govt/Pvt Sector/Self Employed.
- **Note** : Serving member of the Regular Army/Navy/Air Force/ Police /GREF/Para Military and like forces are not eligible.

EMBODIMENT FOR TRAINING
- **One month basic training** in the **first year** of commission.
- **Two months annual training camp every year** including the first year.
- **Three months Post Commissioning training** within first **two years** at IMA Dehradun.

- Date of written Exam : 02 Aug 2015
- Syllabus:-
  - PART I - Essay writing & comprehension (In English).
  - PART II - Objective type question on General Awareness, issues related to Political/Economic, Current Affairs (both national & International), Mental Aptitude, English Grammar & Reasoning.

TERMS AND CONDITIONS OF SERVICE
- Commission is granted in the rank of Lieutenant.
- **Pay and Allowances** and privileges will be **same as Regular Army Officers** when embodied for training and military service.
- **Promotions upto Lt Col by time scale** subject to fulfilling laid down criteria. **Promotion to Colonel and Brigadier by selection.**
- Officers commissioned in Infantry TA may be called out for military service for longer duration depending on the requirement.
- Pay Scales.

RANK	PAY BANDS / SCALE	GRADE PAY	Military Service Pay
LIEUTENANT	PB-3/15600-39100	5400	6000
CAPTAIN	PB-3/15600-39100	6100	6000
MAJOR	PB-3/15600-39100	6600	6000
LT COLONEL	PB-4/37400-67000	8000	6000
COLONEL	PB-4/37400-67000	8700	6000
BRIGADIER	PB-4/37400-67000	8900	6000

CIVILIAN CANDIDATES

HOW TO APPLY. All desirous civilian candidates can obtain **Application Form**, from **Employment Newspaper** or download from www.indianarmy.nic.in (FREE OF COST) and send it alongwith **self addressed stamped envelope of 28 x12 cms size, two passport size photographs** and **postal stamps** worth **Rs.27/-** affixed on envelope (No other cost for submission) to the respective TA Group Headquarters as per the choice of following examination centres. **NO OTHER DOCUMENTS TO BE ATTACHED WITH APPLICATION FORM.**

SER NO	WRITTEN EXAMINATION CENTRE	APPLICATION TO BE SUBMITTED TO
1.	Chandigarh	PIB Cell, TA Group Headquarters, Western Command, Building No.750, Sector-8B, Chandigarh-160 009. Ph No. 0172-2547864
2.	Lucknow & Patna	PIB Cell, TA Group Headquarters Central Command, Lucknow (UP) – 226002. Ph No.0522-2482278
3.	Kolkata & Shillong	PIB Cell, TA Group Headquarters, Eastern Command, Fort William,Kolkata (WB) - 700021. Ph No.033-22313227
4.	Jaipur, Pune, Bangaluru & Hyderabad	PIB Cell, TA Group Headquarters Southern Command, Pune-411001. Ph No. 7768003601, 02026880123
5.	Udhampur & Srinagar	PIB Cell, TA Group Headquarters Northern Command, Udhampur (J&K) – 182101 Ph No.01992 243592

SELECTION PROCEDURE

FOR CIVILIAN CANDIDATES

- Candidates whose application forms are found correct will be called for screening (written exam and interview) by a Preliminary Interview Board (PIB) by the respective TA Group Headquarters.
- Successful candidates will further undergo a Service Selection Board (SSB) and Medical Board for final selection.

FOR EX SERVICE OFFICERS (COMMISSIONED OFFICERS ONLY)

- Ex Service Officers of three services should send their applications alongwith release order and release medical board proceedings directly to Addl Directorate General TA, Integrated HQ of MoD (Army), 'L' Block, Church Road, New Delhi-01.
- The candidates will be screened by an Army HQ Selection Board (ASB) held at Addl Dte Gen TA, GS Branch, 'L' Block, Church Road, New Delhi. Recommended candidate will be required to undergo Medical Examination at Armed Forces Clinic, New Delhi and submit Police Verification Form.

NOTE : Candidate who qualify in written test of PIB/ASB are required to bring the following documents in original alongwith attested copies at the time of interview:-

- All educational qualification certificates (Matric onwards).
- Latest physical fitness certificate from a registered MBBS Doctor.
- Copy of Identity proof with photographs (Voter ID/PAN Card/Passport/Driving license etc).
- Domicile/Residential proof certificate.
- Certificate for proof of age (Matric/Senior Secondary mark sheet & certificate for verification of date of birth).
- Service certificate by candidates employed in Central Govt/Union Territory/State/Semi Govt/Private Sector Authenticated by Head Office alongwith NOC by the department as per format given below.
- Self employed candidates are required to submit an Affidavit on Non-Judicial stamp paper of minimum value duly attested stating nature of employment and annual income alongwith photocopy of PAN card.
- In case of candidates whose names vary in documents submitted, such candidates should submit an affidavit on judicial stamp paper declaring the correct name. The same must be published in newspaper and submit the newspaper cutting alongwith the affidavit.
- Employees of Railways are required to submit NOC authenticated by Railway Board.

NOTE : THE FOLLOWING APPLICABLE CERTIFICATE BE COMPULSORILY PRODUCED AT THE TIME OF INTERVIEW

- **CERTIFICATE TO BE RENDERED BY CANDIDATES EMPLOYED IN CENTRAL GOVT/UNION TERRITORY/STATE GOVT/SEMI GOVT DULY AUTHENTICATED BY HEAD OF OFFICE**

  ➤ I certify that Shri _____ S/o _____ employed under me as _____ for the last _____ yrs and that his character as far as known to me is good. He is/is not recommended for the grant of commission in TA. It is also certified that Shri _____ will be made available for Trg/embodiment for service of the Territorial Army as and when required. It is further certified that Shri _____ does not hold and/or is not likely to hold in the foreseeable future a key–post in _____ (Department/Organisation which could affect the minimum essential functions of this Department/Organisation. However, in the event of this becoming a key man subsequently the Additional Director General Territorial Army, New Delhi shall be requested immediately to release or discharge him from the Territorial Army.
  Place _____ Signature _____
  Date _____ Designation _____
  Stamp/Seal of Office _____

- **CERTIFICATE TO BE RENDERED BY SELF EMPLOYED PERSONAL TO BE AUTHENTICATED BY GAZETTED/COMMISSIONED OFFICER/DM**

  ➤ Certify that Shri _____ S/o _____ is known to me for the last _____ years and bears good moral character to the best of my belief and knowledge. He is/is not recommended for the grant of commission in the TA.
  Place _____ Signature _____
  Date _____ Designation _____
  Stamp/Seal of Office _____

- **CETIFICATE TO BE RENDERED BY CANDIDATES EMPLOYED IN PRIVATE SECTOR (TO BE AUTHENTICATED BY HEAD OF OFFICE)**

  ➤ Certified that any difference between the civil and military pay and allowances of the applicant Name _____ S/o _____ an employee of this organization will be paid by us for the period of his military duties in the Territorial Army. On return from military duty in the Territorial Army Shri _____ will be absorbed in the same or equivalent post which he would have held if his service in the civil had not been so interrupted and the such military service would count for all benefits in his civil job, like seniority for promotion, increment of pay, bonus and provident fund etc. To which he would have otherwise been entitled.
  Place _____ Signature _____
  Date _____ Designation _____
  Stamp/Seal of Office _____

LAST DATE: Form completed in all respects will be accepted till 30 Jun 2015 at respective Territorial Army Group Headquarters.

For more details about TA visit us at www.indianarmy.gov.in and download **APPLICATION FORM** (FREE OF COST). **This is the only authentic website of TA.**

INCOMPLETE APPLICATION FORM WILL BE REJECTED WITHOUT INTIMATION

APPLICATION FORM FOR COMMISSION IN THE TERRITORIAL ARMY FOR NON DEPT (INF) TA

1. Candidate's Name																	Self-attested photograph of the candidate size 4.5x 3.5 cms (To be pasted)

To be filled in BLOCK CAPITALS in blue ball point pen.

2. Father's Name															

3. Permanent Address	House No				Block/Pkt	
	Village/Town				Post Office	
	Tehsil				District	
	State				Pin Code	
	e mail				Telephone No	

4. Present Address	House No				Block/Pkt	
	Village/Town				Post Office	
	Tehsil				District	
	State				Pin Code	
	Mobile No				Land Line No.	

4 (a) Choice of written exam centre : Chandigarh-01   Lucknow - 02   Patna-03   Kolkata   - 04   Shillong-05
Pune   -06   Bangalore-07   Jaipur - 08   Hyderabad-09   Udhampur - 10
Srinagar   -11

5. Date of Birth as given in Matric Certificate	6. Gender (Strike out whichever is not applicable)	7. No of attempts already made in SSB for :-
Day **Month** **Year**	M F	NDA CDSE TA

8. Educational Qualification	9. Educational Stream	10. Nationality
Code : Graduation - 01 Post Graduation - 02	Code : Arts – 01, Science – 02, Commerce – 03, Engineering – 04 Medical – 05, MBA – 06 & Any other – 07	

11. Marital Status :	12. Next of Kin	12 (a). Name of next of kin
Code : Single -01 Married – 02 Divorced - 03	Code : Father – 01, Mother – 02, Wife- 03, Son – 04, Daughter – 05 & Other - 06	

13. Nature of employment with code	Code : Central Govt/Union Territory - 01 State Govt/Semi Govt - 02 Self Employed - 03 Pvt Sector - 04

FOR EX SERVICE OFFICERONLY

14.   Details of previous commissioned service in the Armed Forces (Attach copy of Release Order & Release Medical Board proceedings) (write code wherever applicable).

(a)	Service		Code : Army-01, Air Force-02, Navy-03, TA-04	
(b)	Substantive Rank		(c)	Service Number	
(d)	Date of commission		(e)	Date of Retirement	
(f)	Arms / Service & Unit		(g)	Medical Category at the time of release	

15.	Reason for Discharge		Code :	Med Bd Out - 01 Voluntary Discharge - 02 Disciplinary Ground - 03 On Superannuation - 04 Resignation - 05 Any Other -06

16. **DECLARATION**.

➢ In the event of my selection for commission in the Territorial Army, I am willing to serve anywhere in India for longer duration also, whenever required, or as per the rules and orders in force from time to time.

➢ I clearly understand that if at any time during the period of probation I am not found suitable, I shall have to resign my commission in accordance with the rules and orders in force from time to time and in case I decline to do so I am liable to be discharged/removed from the Territorial Army.

➢ I am fully aware that if it is found at any stage that I have knowingly furnished any details which is/are false or have suppressed material information or I fail to comply with the above undertakings, my candidature will be rejected summarily and if already commissioned, I shall be liable to be discharged/removed from the Territorial Army.

Signature of candidate

Annexure II (Year 2020)

JOIN TERRITORIAL ARMY AS AN OFFICER
(ONLY FOR EX ARMED FORCES COMMISSIONED OFFICERS)
PART TIME COMMITMENT AND NOT A FULL TIME CAREER !

ARMY HEADQUARTERS SELECTION BOARD (ASB) - 2020
(DATE OF INTERVIEW: APRIL 2020)
(LAST DATE FOR RECEIPT OF APPLICATION: 31 JANUARY 2020)
(Territorial Army Official Website : www.jointerritorialarmy.gov.in)

Applications are invited from gainfully employed Ex Armed Forces Commissioned Officers for an opportunity of donning the uniform and serving the Nation as Territorial Army Officers (Non Departmental), based on the concept of enabling motivated Ex Service Officers to serve in a military environment without having to sacrifice their primary professions. You can serve the Nation in two capacities – as a civilian and as a soldier. No other option allows you such an expense of experiences

1. CONDITIONS OF ELIGIBILITY :

(a) Only Ex Service Officer can apply.

(b) **Nationality :** Only citizen of India (male and female).

(c) **Age Limits :** 18 to 42 years on the date of application.

(d) **Educational Qualifications :** Graduate from recognized university.

(e) **Physical Standards :** A candidate must be physically and medically fit in all respects.

(f) **Employment :** Gainfully Employed.

Note : Serving member of the Regular Army/ Navy/ Air Force/ Police/ GREF/ Para Military and like forces are not eligible.

2. DATE OF INTERVIEW : APRIL 2020 (Firm dates will be communicated later by post).

3. LAST DATE OF RECEIPT OF APPLICATION : Application form completed in all respects will be accepted till 31 JANUARY 2020 at Additional Directorate General Territorial Army, Integrated Headquarters of Ministry of Defence, 'L' Block, Church Road, New Delhi – 110 001.

4. The date of holding the Interview as mentioned above is liable to be changed at the discretion of the competent authority.

5. **Ex Service Officers to ensure their eligibility for the examination :** The Ex Service Officers applying for the ASB Interview should ensure that they fulfill all eligibility conditions for admission to the Interview. Their admission at all the stages of the Interview will be purely provisional subject to satisfying the prescribed eligibility conditions. Mere issue of Admission certificate to the Ex Service Officers will not imply that their candidature has been finally cleared by the competent authority.

6. Type of Exam: Only Interview.

7. HOW TO APPLY. All desirous Ex Service Officers (Commissioned Officers only) of three services can download Application Form (IAF (TA)-9 (Revised) Part - 1) from www.jointerritorialarmy.gov.in (FREE OF COST) and send applications alongwith Photocopy of Release Order and Photocopy of Release Medical Board Proceedings to Additional Directorate General Territorial Army, Integrated Headquarters of Ministry of Defence, 'L' Block, Church Road, New Delhi – 110 001.

8. Ex Service Officer should note that no request for change of date of Interview will be granted.

9. The eligible candidates shall be issued a call up letter and will be sent by post by the Territorial Army Directorate.

10. SELECTION PROCEDURE :

(a) The Ex Service Officers will be screened by the Army Headquarters Selection Board (ASB) held at Additional Directorate General Territorial Army, Integrated Headquarters of Ministry of Defence, 'L' Block, Church Road, New Delhi – 110 001.

(b) Recommended Ex Service Officers will undergo Medical Examination at Armed Forces Clinic, New Delhi followed by their Police Verification for final selection.

(c) Vacancies for male and female candidates will be determined as per organizational requirement.

11. EMBODIMENT FOR TRAINING:

(a) One month Basic Training in the first year of commission.

(b) Two months Annual Training Camp every year including the first year.

12. TERMS AND CONDITIONS OF SERVICE :

(a) Territorial Army is part time concept with mandatory two months training in a year and does not provide full time career.

(b) Service in Territorial Army do not guarantee pension and the same is subject to embodied service as per organisational requirement.

(c) Commission is granted in the rank of Lieutenant.

(d) Pay and Allowances and privileges will be same as Regular Army Officers when embodied for training and military service.

(e) Promotions upto Lt Col by time scale subject to fulfilling laid down criteria. Promotion to Colonel and Brigadier by selection.

(f) Officers commissioned in Infantry TA may be called out for military service for longer duration depending on the requirement.

(g) Once previous service is verified from concerned PCDA (O) they are granted Ante-Date Seniority for Pay and Promotion.

(h) Pay Scales (VIIth CPC):

RANK	LEVEL	PAY MATRIX	Military Service Pay
LIEUTENANT	Level 10	56,100 - 1,77,500	15500/-
CAPTAIN	Level 10A	6,13,00 - 1,93,900	15500/-
MAJOR	Level 11	6,94,00 - 2,07,200	15500/-
LT COLONEL	Level 12A	1,21,200 - 2,12400	15500/-
COLONEL	Level 13	1,30,600 - 2,15,900	15500/-
BRIGADIER	Level 13A	1,39,600 - 2,17,600	15500/-

13. Ex Service Officers are required to bring the following documents in original alongwith self attested copies at the time of interview. All those ex service officers whose complete documents are not produced for verifications will not be allowed to attend the interview.

(a) Application Form IAF (TA)-9 (Revised) Part-2 to be downloaded from www.jointerritorialarmy.gov.in and filled up in their own hand writing.

(b) All educational qualification certificates (Matric onwards).

(c) Latest physical fitness certificate from a registered MBBS Doctor.

(d) Copy of Identity proof with photographs (Voter ID/PAN Card/Aadhar Card/Passport/Driving license etc).

(e) Domicile/ Residential proof.

(f) Certificate for proof of age (Matric/ Senior Secondary mark sheet & certificate for verification of date of birth).

(g) Service certificate by candidates employed in Central Govt/ Union Territory/ State/Semi Govt/ Private Sector Authenticated by Head of office alongwith No Objection Certificate by the department as per format given at Para 14 (a) below.

(h) Self employed candidates are required to submit an Affidavit on Non-Judicial stamp paper of minimum value duly attested stating nature of employment and annual income alongwith photocopy of PAN card and self certified character certificate.

(j) Ex Service Officers whose names vary in documents should submit copy of Gazette notification of India/ State showing the correct name duly supported by newspaper cuttings.

(k) Copy of Release Order.

(l) Copy of Release Medical Board Proceedings.

(m) Latest income proof from the appropriate authority (i.e. Income Tax Revenue Department / Magistrate / Employer).

(n) Copy of PAN Card.

(o) Copy of Aadhar Card.

(p) Copy of Certificates / Reports of all Courses.

(q) Discharge / Service Particular Booklet.

(r) Copy of latest Income Tax Return (ITR) filed.

14. THE FOLLOWING APPLICABLE CERTIFICATE BE COMPULSORILY PRODUCED AT THE TIME OF INTERVIEW:

(a) CERTIFICATE TO BE RENDERED BY CANDIDATES EMPLOYED IN CENTRAL GOVT/UNION TERRITORY/ STATE GOVT/ SEMI GOVT DULY AUTHENTICATED BY HEAD OF OFFICE

I certify that Shri/Smt/Kumari _____ S/o D/o W/o _____ employed under me as _____for the last _____ yrs and that their character as far as known to me is good. He/She is/is not recommended for the grant of commission in Territorial Army. It is also certified that Shri/Smt/Kumari____will be made available for Trg/embodiment for service of the Territorial Army as and when required. It is further certified that Shri/Smt/Kumari _____ does not hold and/or is not likely to hold in the foreseeable future a key–post in _____ (Department/ Organisation) which could affect the minimum essential functions of this Department/ Organisation. However, in the event of him/her becoming a key person subsequently the Additional Director General Territorial Army, New Delhi shall be requested immediately to release or discharge him/her from the Territorial Army.

Place _____ Signature

Date _____ Designation

Stamp/Seal of Office

(b) CERTIFICATE TO BE RENDERED BY SELF EMPLOYED PERSONNEL (SELF CERTIFIED BY THE CANDIDATE)

(i) I _____ (Name) S/o D/o W/o _____ certify that I possess good moral character to the best of my belief and knowledge.

Place _____ Signature

Date _____ Name

(ii) Affidavit on Non-Judicial stamp paper of minimum value duly endorsed by notary. I_____ (Name) S/o D/o W/o _____ resident of _____ do hereby solemnly affirm and declare as follows:–

(a) That I am a resident of above address.

(b) That I am self employed as _____.

(c) That my annual income from all sources is approximately Rs _____. The above statement is true and correct to the best of my knowledge and belief.

Deponent

Verification : Verified at _____ on this _____ day of _____ 20___ that the contents of above affidavit are true to my knowledge & belief and nothing has been concealed therein.

Deponent

(c) CERTIFICATE TO BE RENDERED BY CANDIDATES EMPLOYED IN PRIVATE SECTOR (TO BE AUTHENTICATED BY HEAD OF OFFICE)

Certified that any difference between the civil and military pay and allowances of the applicant Name _____ S/o D/o W/o _____ an employee of this organization will be paid by us for the period of his/her military duties in the Territorial Army. On return from military duty in the Territorial Army Shri/Smt/Kumari_____ will be absorbed in the same or equivalent post which he/she would have held if his/her service in the civil had not been so interrupted and the such military service would count for all benefits in his/her civil job, like seniority for promotion, increment of pay, bonus and provident fund etc. To which he/she would have otherwise been entitled.

Place _____ Signature

Date _____ Designation

Stamp/ Seal of Office

15. LAST DATE: Form completed in all respects will be accepted till 31 JANUARY 2020 at Additional Directorate General Territorial Army, Integrated Headquarters of Ministry of Defence, 'L' Block, Church Road, New Delhi – 110 001. For more details about Territorial Army visit us at www.jointerritorialarmy.gov.in and download APPLICATION FORM (FREE OF COST). This is the only authentic website of Territorial Army.

16. INCOMPLETE/ INELIGIBLE APPLICATION FORM AND THOSE APPLICATION FORM RECEIVED AFTER 31 JANUARY 2020 WILL BE REJECTED WITHOUT INTIMATION.

17. APPLICATION FORM OF CIVILIAN CANDIDATES WILL NOT BE ACCEPTED AND WILL BE REJECTED WITHOUT INTIMATION.

CPSIA information can be obtained
at www.ICGtesting.com
Printed in the USA
LVHW030455260122
709358LV00001B/26